YEAROS DVASH

יערות דבש

TWO *DERASHOS*
from
YEAROS DVASH
by
Rabbi Yonason Eybeshutz

Translated and Annotated by
Rabbi Avraham Yaakov Finkel

YESHIVATH BETH MOSHE
SCRANTON, PA.

THIS VOLUME

IS LOVINGLY DEDICATED

לעילוי נשמת

אִיסֶר ב״ר פייבוש ז״ל

BY HIS FAMILY

IN APPRECIATION OF HIS CARE

AND

FOR BEING SUCH A MEANINGFUL

PART OF THEIR LIVES

חזית איש מהיר במלאכתו לפני מלכים יתיצב

הולך תמים ופועל צדק ודובר אמת בלבבו

נפטר י״א ניסן תשע״א

תנצב״ה

CONTENTS

PROLOGUE   vii

SUMMARY OF PROLOGUE   ix

TRANSLATOR'S INTRODUCTION   xi

FIRST *DERASHA*   1

  I: THE TEN DAYS OF TESHUVAH   3

  II: FIGHTING THE YETZER HARA
       THROUGH TORAH STUDY   8

  III: THE POWER OF TESHUVAH   18

  IV: THE *SHEMONEH ESREI*   32

      The First Berachah
      SHIELD OF AVRAHAM   33

      The Second Berachah
      REVIVAL OF THE DEAD   34

      The Third Berachah
      THE HOLINESS OF G-D   35

      The Fourth Berachah
      GRANTING KNOWLEDGE   37

      The Fifth Berachah
      TESHUVAH   44

      The Sixth Berachah
      FORGIVENESS   46

      The Seventh Berachah
      REDEEMER OF YISRAEL   47

      The Eighth Berachah
      HEALING AND RECOVERY   49

      The Ninth Berachah
      BLESSING THE PRODUCE OF THE YEAR   52

The Tenth Berachah
INGATHERING OF THE EXILES   55

The Eleventh Berachah
RESTORATION OF JUSTICE   59

The Twelfth Berachah
DENOUNCING REBELLIOUS SINNERS   61

The Thirteenth Berachah
BLESSING THE RIGHTEOUS   66

The Fourteenth Berachah
REBUILDING YERUSHALAYIM   68

The Fifteenth Berachah
THE GLORY OF SALVATION   68

The Sixteenth Berachah
LISTENING TO OUR PRAYERS   69

The Seventeenth Berachah
RESTORATION OF THE DIVINE PRESENCE TO TZION   70

The Eighteenth Berachah
THANKSGIVING   72

The Nineteenth Berachah
PEACE   72

    V: RABBI ELAZAR BEN DORDAYA'S TESHUVAH   78

SIXTH *DERASHA*   85

    I: THE TWO GOATS   87

    II: THE DAY OF JUDGMENT   106

GLOSSARY   113

הקדמה
מראש הישיבה
מורינו הרב יעקב שניידמאן שליט"א

הספר יערות דבש הוא מן הספרים המיוחדים שכלול בו
ביאורים בהרבה מאמרי חז"ל הסתומים, ובביאור המאמרים מבאר
יסודות באמונה ובבטחון. הספר נתקבל בכל תפוצות ישראל ואין
צורך להאריך בחשיבותו. בדרוש שהעתקנו מבאר כוונות יסודיות
בברכת שמונה עשרה, וגם יסודות גדולות בדרך עבודה.

תפלה היא עמוד העבודה, ובאמת אף בזמן הבית לא היתה
עבודת הקרבנות בערך כח התפלה. והמחבר בעצמו כותב וז"ל
אשרי האיש המתפלל בכוונת הלב י"ח ברכות, וזה יותר לרצון לפני
ה' מזבח ומנחה עכ"ל והרבה ישועות באו לכלל ישראל ע"י
תפלתם. ובעת קריעת ים סוף אמרו חז"ל והובא ברש"י שמות פרק
יד' ויצעקו – תפשו אומנות אבותם. וכן חנה זכה לשמואל בעיקר
ע"י תפלתה, ודוד המלך אמר כי לא תחפץ זבח ואתנה עולה לא
תרצה: זבחי אלהים רוח נשברה לב נשבר ונדכה אלהים לא תבזה:
פירוש, עיקר הכפרה הוא הלב שיש לו להקב"ה בתפלתו. ואין
הכוונה ח"ו שאין מקום לקרבנות רק דיסוד הכפרה והרצון הוא
שפיכת הנפש ע"י תפלה ותחנונים. והקרבנות בכחם להעלות האדם
למדרגה גבוה, רק אחר התפלה בלב נשבר, לכן אמר דוד המלך
כי לא תחפץ זבח כלומר אם אין לו לב נשבר.

בכוונת תפלה יש כמה מדרגות יש מי שמכוין להמילות לבד
ואף שאינו יודע פירוש המלות עכ"פ הוא מכוין שיתקיים ע"י
דיבורו כל מה שנתכוונו בו אנשכה"ג, ויש מדרגה למעלה מזה
וכמבואר בנפש החיים שכל דיבור שהאדם מוציא מפיו הוא בא
מנפש האדם ונחשב שיש במילה חלק מנפשו, ועפי"ז מכוין שנפשו

יעלה למעלה עם הדיבור. וביאורו, דחז"ל למדו מצות תפלה
מהפסוק ולעבדו בכל לבבכם ובכל נפשכם. ודקדק בנפש החיים
דבשלמא בכל לבבכם פירושו עבודה בלב שזה תפלה, אבל מה
ענין בכל נפשכם. ומבאר דכל מילה הוא חלק מנפש האדם וע"י
אמירתו עולה נפשו למעלה להתדבק בקב"ה. וזה נמי שייך אפי'
בלא ידיעה בפירוש המלות. למעלה מזה שמכוין כונה של העלאת
הנפש עם ידיעתו בפירוש המלות. למעלה מזה שמכוין יותר
מפירוש המלות, והיינו שמכוין להענינים שנתבארו בדרוש
שהעתקנו מהיערות דבש, למעלה מזה שמכוין לסודות שיש בכל
ברכה, לצירופי שמות שמכוון כנגד כל עולם ועולם, אשרי מי
שזכה לכך.

ואף שהזמן שאנו נותנים להתפלל מספיק רק לכוין פירוש
המלות, מ"מ נראה שתבוא תועלת גדולה בתפילתו על ידי לימוד
הענינים שנתבארו בדרוש זה. דאף שאינו מכוין כוונות אלו בתוך
תפלתו, מ"מ אם קודם שעומד להתפלל מכוין להתפלל עפ"י כל
הכוונות שלמד בדרוש זה הוי מעלה גדולה. ועוד נראה שיש אופן
שיכול לכוין בהדיא. ולמשל בפירוש ברכת השנים, מבאר ר' יהונתן
שאכילתו יהא בטהרה, והיינו שלא יהא מעורב איסור במאכל
ועוד שיאכל בטהרה ולא מתוך ניבול פה לה"ר ומושב לצים, ואם
אין אדם נזהר בזה נכנס באדם רוח טומאה ע"י אכילתו. והוא
מבאר זה באריכות, ואחר שאדם לומד זה יכול לעשות מזה
מחשבה קצרה, והוא שיתפלל בברכת השנים שמזונותיו יהא
בטהרה עפ"י מה שלמד, ועי"ז חשוב כאילו כיוון לכל מה שנתבאר
שם. וכן יכול לעשות כוונה קצרה בכל ברכה.

חז"ל אמרו דתפלה הוא בכלל דברים העומדים ברומו של
עולם ובנ"א מזלזלים בהם. והוא כפשוטו, שהדברים עולים לרומו
של עולם לפעול, וכבר ביארנו דהדברים הם ממש נפש האדם
שעולה למעלה, והוא ממש כמו הקרבת קרבן שמקריב עצמו
בשעת תפלה. ובנ"א מזלזלים בהם שאינם יודעים חשיבות הדיבור
ומה שיכול לפעול. הרחמן הוא יסייענו להיות מן היודעים חשיבות
התפלה, ונזכה להתדבק להקב"ה ע"י תפלתנו.

SUMMARY OF
RABBI YAAKOV SCHNAIDMAN'S PROLOGUE

The Sefer *Yearos Devash* is unique in its ability to teach many fundamental principles of faith while explaining cryptic passages of the Sages. It is not necessary to comment on the value of this sefer, as it has been accepted by all of Yisrael.

Fundamental ideas in serving Hashem and an in-depth interpretation of the *shemoneh esrei* prayer are included in the *derashos* that we have translated here.

Prayer is the cornerstone of service to Hashem. Even the *korbanos* brought in the Beis Hamikdash did not compare to prayer, as the *Shulchan Aruch* says, "Praiseworthy is he who prays the *shemoneh esrei* with proper concentration; this is more pleasing to Hashem than sacrifices and meal offerings."

David Hamelech said, *You did not desire a sacrifice... Rather the offering to Hashem is a broken spirit; a broken heart will not be looked down upon by G-d*. Atonement is achieved through the heart, which prays to G-d. Although the sacrifices are important, atonement comes only after one prays with a broken heart.

Many salvations came to the Bnei Yisrael through prayer. We were saved at the *Yam Suf* when we followed the path of our ancestors who prayed in their time of need. Chana merited giving birth to Shemuel the prophet through her prayers.

One can pray on many levels. Those who pray, saying the words although they do not understand them, hope to achieve whatever the Men of the Great Assembly had in mind for each prayer.

Rabbi Yaakov Schnaidman is the Rosh Yeshivah of Yeshivath Beth Moshe Scranton, Pennsylvania.

Onkelos translates, *And (G-d) breathed into his nostrils a spirit of life (Bereishis 2:7)*, to mean G-d gave man the power of speech, proving that speech emanates from the soul; when one prays it is as if he gives his soul to G-d through the words of his prayer. Thus, with the second level of prayer, if one's every word comes from his soul, he hopes to be considered as if he were ascending to heaven, as explained in *Sefer Nefesh HaChaim*.

The third level of prayer is reached by one who understands the words he is saying, while an even higher level is reserved for one who thinks about ideas such as those expressed in *Sefer Yearos Dvash*. Those who have the esoteric meaning of each *berachah* in mind are praying on a very high level.

Although, with the limited time we have for prayer, we cannot think of more than the simple translation of the words, our prayers can still benefit from the lessons taught in this volume, for if one prays thinking to include all the thoughts that he learned from this sefer, they will be included in his prayer. However, one can do even better than that. For instance, in the *berachah* of Sustenance, the *Yearos Devash* gives a lengthy exposition about eating in purity. One must eat kosher food and avoid gossip and frivolity while eating, but if one is not careful, he can become contaminated through the food he eats even if it is kosher. If, while praying, one has a synopsis of this in mind, planning to eat in purity, it will be considered as if he thought all the ideas expressed in the sefer. With this in mind he can greatly elevate his prayers.

Our Sages said: Prayer is one of the things that stand at the height of the world, yet people are careless about it. This is literally true, for the words of prayer actually rise to the heights of heaven. The words of prayer include the soul of man, so it is considered as if he offered himself on high, yet people don't realize what they are accomplishing.

May the Merciful One help us to become aware of the importance of prayer, and bring us close to Him through prayer.

TRANSLATOR'S INTRODUCTION

⸺◈⸺

The *sefer Yaros Dvash* is a highly regarded and widely quoted collection of sermons by the illustrious Rabbi Yonasan Eybeshutz. The present volume contains sermons for the month of Ellul and the *Yamim Nora'im*. The *derashos* reflect the profound wisdom of Rabbi Yonasan, his incredible range and depth of knowledge and his devotion to his community, his students, and Klal Yisrael.

Of particular interest is Rabbi Yonasan's perceptive insight into the workings of the human psyche, the spiritual source of man's strengths and weaknesses. He astutely pinpoints the schemes used by the *yetzer hara* to entice us and lead us astray, offering strategies for overcoming its nefarious designs.

Most enlightening is Rabbi Yonasan's *peirush* in the first sermon on the *berachos* of the weekday *shemoneh esrei*. In his comments, interspersed with profound kabbalistic insights, he explains the deeper meaning of each *berachah* and describes the thoughts we should have in mind when reciting the *berachah*.

One of his main themes is that we should not attribute our fortune or misfortune to chance, but understand that our destiny is governed by Hashem. Sincere prayer is effective, for Hashem is the *shomei'a tefillah*, "the One, who hears prayer."

BIOGRAPHICAL NOTES

Rabbi Yonasan Eybeshutz (Cracow—1690, Altona—1764) was an illustrious Talmudic and Halachic scholar as well as a great Kabbalist. In 1715 he became *rosh yeshivah* in Prague, and in 1736 he was appointed *dayan* in Prague where he was held in high esteem. In 1741, he became rabbi of the prosperous *kehillah* of Metz, France, where he led a yeshivah that attracted students from far and wide. He was venerated for his sermons which lasted six or seven hours, drawing massive attentive audiences.

In 1730 Rabbi Yonasan was elected chief rabbi of the prominent "Three Kehillos" Altona, Hamburg, and Wandsbeck, popularly called by their acronym *kehillos AHU*. Unfortunately, a bitter controversy erupted between Rabbi Yonasan and Rabbi Yaakov Emden, a long-time rabbi in Altona, eventually dividing all of European Jewry into two opposing camps.

The root of the conflict was the fact that Rabbi Yonasan had written *kamei'os* (amulets) to be worn by pregnant women. At that time sixteen pregnant women in the Metz region had miscarried shortly before giving birth, and in the merit of Rabbi Yonasan the scourge stopped. Evil tongues spread fraudulent rumors that Rabbi Yonasan's *kamei'os* contained references to Shabsai Tzvi, the false mashiach. This fueled a deplorable wave of malice against Rabbi Yonansan.

Rabbi Yonasan was a prolific writer. Thirty of his works on Halachah and *drush* (homiletics) have been published, including *Urim Vetummim, Kreisi Upleisi, Sar Ha'elef, Binah Le'ittim*, and the famous *Yaaros Dvash*.

The title *Yaaros Dvash*, "Forest of Honey," is a play on the author's name, Yonasan, mentioned in the verse, *Yonasan dipped his stick into the* "yaaros dvash," *forest of honey, and his eyes lit up* (1 *Shemuel* 14:27). Reading this *sefer*, the reader's eyes will surely light up with the inspiring thoughts and novel insights of Rabbi Yonasan Eybeschutz, *zechuso yagain aleinu*.

Avraham Yaakov Finkel
Tammuz 5772/'12

YEAROS DVASH

First Derasha

I: THE TEN DAYS OF TESHUVAH

Yeshayah the prophet says, *Seek Hashem when He can be found.*[1] Expounding this verse, the Gemara[2] asks, "And when can a person find G-d?"

The Gemara answers, "During the ten days between Rosh Hashanah and Yom Kippur, for these ten days are auspicious for *teshuvah.*"

[G-d's willingness to accept our *teshuvah*] demonstrates His kindness, revealing how greatly He desires the well being of His people. Since these days are designated for *teshuvah*, whoever spends them absorbed in *tefillah* and *teshuvah* is to be commended. In fact, the Arizal says these days [are so special] we should consider them as *Chol Hamoed*[3] days, refraining from conducting any business or work, unless it would cause us monetary loss; rather, we should spend our time scrutinizing our conduct.

Heeding my own counsel, I will not expound at length on scriptural verses; rather I will attempt to inspire you toward greater piety and devotion.

RAIN AND DEW

Praiseworthy is the person who values G-d's goodness, recognizing how He rouses the sleepers and spurs the

---

1   *Yeshayah* 55:6
2   *Rosh Hashanah* 18a.
3   The intermediate days of the holidays when work is restricted.

slumberous to do *teshuvah*, as we read in the Gemara:[4]
Yisrael said, *Let us strive to know Hashem . . . that He may
come to us like the rain*.[5]

Hashem replied, "My daughter, you asked for rain that
falls intermittently, sometimes falling and sometimes not
falling. However I will act like dew that falls continually, as it
says, *I will be to Yisrael like the dew*.[6]

Rain and dew are different. Scientists agree that rainfall occurs when particles of moisture rise to the upper atmosphere.
There, the moisture condenses into droplets of water; eventually these droplets can no longer be suspended in the air,
causing rain. When the earth is dry and no water vapor rises,
rain does not fall. Dew, on the other hand, is not caused by
moisture rising from earth. It originates from particles of
water floating in the frigid stratosphere. When the sun warms
the cold particles, droplets are formed that descend to the
earth as dew. As a result, dew falls continuously, and there
never is a lack of it.

TAKING THE INITIATIVE

The same is true about *teshuvah*. [Like rain drops which
form from moisture on earth rising aloft,] *teshuvah* starts
with a small stimulus down on earth [triggered by a person
doing *teshuvah*.] This prompts G-d to help him, as the Sages
say, *A person who comes to purify himself is helped from Above*.[7]
However, he must take the first step. In the same vein the
Medrash says: [G-d says,] *Make for Me an opening as small as
the eye of a needle, and I will open for you a gate as wide as the*

---

4   *Taanis* 4b.
5   *Hoshea* 6:3
6   *Hoshea* 14:6
7   *Yoma* 30b

portal of the Sanctuary.[8] These sayings emphasize that man must take the initiative.

G-d Sends Blessing
Without a Prior Stimulus

However, if—G-d forbid—Yisrael does not do *teshuvah,* they will be redeemed nonetheless, for G-d sends His stream of abundance [like dew] even without stimulus from below, saying, *For My sake, for My own sake do I act.*[9] He will pour out His kindness to cleanse the people's hearts without any arousal from below.

This occurred at the time of Creation when there was no activity down on earth, as it says, *There was no man to work the soil.*[10] Hashem created the world [even without a stimulus from below.] The same will happen in time to come; [G-d will cleanse people's hearts even if they don't do *teshuvah*]. This is why G-d promised dew rather than rain when Yisrael asked for rain. Yisrael assumed that G-d would not send down His flow of abundance without the prior impulse of *teshuvah.* Yisrael asked, *that He may come to us like the rain* in response to our *teshuvah.* Since Yisrael did *teshuvah* haphazardly, they expected G-d to scatter His blessings here and there, bit by bit, like a sprinkle of tiny raindrops.

But G-d replied, "You are asking for a sprinkle that falls only now and then because you assume you are not worthy of a downpour, but I will act the way I did at the time of Creation, providing your needs even without a stimulus on your part. This is the meaning of *I will be to Yisrael like dew,* it originates above and is always present, without the need for vapors to rise from the earth to stimulate it.

---

[8] Shir HaShirim Rabbah 5:3
[9] *Yeshayah* 48:11
[10] *Bereishis* 2:5

HASHEM BECKONS

R osh Hashanah is the annual reenactment of Creation, as we say in the prayer of *Mussaf*: *Today is the birthday of the world*. This being so, the Ten Days of Teshuvah inspire us to do *teshuvah* without prior stimulus from our actions. G-d Himself impels us to do *teshuvah,* similar to Creation which took place without prior inducement, and like the dew that descends without the catalyst of moisture rising from earth. Thus it says, *Seek Hashem when He can be found*—Hashem makes Himself accessible even before we appeal to Him. On the contrary, He appeals to us to do *teshuvah.* Therefore, during these Ten Days, a thoughtful person feels drawn to *teshuvah* and the fear of Heaven. Because Hashem beckons us, our hearts yearn for *teshuvah* even if we are distracted by mundane concerns. When Hashem is calling, how can we turn a deaf ear?

RECTIFYING THE SEVEN DAYS OF THE WEEK

T he seven days between Rosh Hashanah and Yom Kippur correspond to the seven days of the week; on each of these seven days we do *teshuvah* for transgressions we committed on that particular day of the week. For example, on Sunday we do *teshuvah* for the sins we did on all our Sundays. We do the same on Monday, and so on, thus rectifying the failings of all our days. Let us examine our deeds, searching for ways to do *teshuvah* according to this program.

Of course, at the close of Yom Kippur, after completing ten days of *teshuvah*, do not think, G-d forbid, that happy days are here again; the time of wine and roses, and the hour of boys mingling with girls can commence. Do not rush headlong like a deer whose leash has been cut, or like a liberated prisoner thinking about inane and rebellious ideas that serve to embolden the powers of evil.

BEWARE OF THE SHEARERS

In the song *Adir Ayom veNora* chanted on *Motza'ei Shabbos* we say, *Save Your flock from the hands of the shearers.* What is the meaning of this request?

Sometimes we will see a sinner do *teshuvah*—fasting, weeping, putting on sackcloth and ashes, and engaging in other devout acts. But after a time, this sinner backslides, forgetting all his admirable deeds. His relapse may be explained with the following analogy: A shepherd, eager to sell wool, feeds his flock salt and various potions that promote the growth of the woolen fleece. Year after year, when the wool is fully-grown, he shears it, bringing it to market.

Satanic forces of evil are nourished by extracting *kedushah* from sinners [through their sins.] What do these forces of evil do? Like the shearers [who feed their sheep only to promote the growth of a luxuriant fleece in order to shear it,] the forces of evil inspire people to return to Hashem and live virtuously so their soul will once again be satiated with G-d's goodness, after they have sinned and lost *kedushah.* Then, after this is accomplished, they parasitically extract his regained *kedushah,* making him abandon his righteous way of life again. Regrettably, the sinner hands over his talents and strength to strangers.

This is the meaning of our plea, *Save Your flock from the hands of the shearers.* We implore Hashem to shield us from such occurrences.

One who repents must prevent himself from reverting to his foolish ways, scrutinizing his character traits and behavior. The only means for improving man's behavior is through Torah, *tefillah*, and the knowledge and fear of G-d. And so, the focus of my sermon today will be Torah and *tefillah.*

II: Fighting the Yetzer Hara through Torah Study

The Gemara[11] says, *If [the yetzer hara,] this loathsome fellow, takes hold of you, drag him into the beis medrash. If he goes, fine. If not, recite the Shema. If that does not help chase him away, remind yourself of the day of death.* This begs the question: Why do we draw out the process of ridding ourselves of the *yetzer hara* [by dragging him first to the Beis Medrash and then reciting the *Shema?*] Why not choose the safest and most efficient path, reminding ourselves of the day of death immediately?

Torah Study to Defeat the *Yetzer Hara*

There are three types of sins, and the primary way to fight the *yetzer hara* [against all these sins] is through Torah study. We can see this from the Gemara[12] that asks, *How do women earn a share in the World to Come?*

[The Gemara answers,] *By waiting for their husbands until they come home from the yeshivah, and by bringing their small children to the synagogue [where they learn Torah].*

The Gemara's question is puzzling. After all, except for the few time dependant mitzvos from which they are exempt, women are obligated to keep all the mitzvos just like men. [Why is it questionable that they earn a share in the World to Come?][13]

---

[11] *Berachos 5a*
[12] *Berachos 17a*
[13] The answer will be given later in the sermon.

8

Mitzvos Lead to Perfection

We know that it is through mitzvos that we reach perfection. Therefore, the Sages of the *Mishnah*[14] say, *The master of the house is insistent, and the wages are great.* The Holy One, blessed be He, urges us to fulfill His mitzvos for our own benefit, so we can earn a rich reward. Like a father who advises his son to use a specific strategy in business, knowing it will bring him success, the Holy One, blessed be He, wanting us to prosper, commands us to keep His mitzvos, for they bring rich reward.

Since Man can attain perfection even with one mitzvah, the *Mishnah*[15] continues: *You are not required to complete the task.* Don't let the *yetzer hara* mislead you into thinking you can only reach perfection by keeping all the mitzvos of the Torah. Using such sophistry, the *yetzer hara* encourages you to weaken your observance, making you think all your effort in serving Hashem is pointless, G-d forbid. But that is not true; no one can keep all the mitzvos. Every mitzvah brings perfection if it is done flawlessly, without an ulterior motive. This is what the Sages had in mind when they said, *You are not required to complete the task.*

To illustrate: A person hired a contractor to build a house for a certain price. If the contractor does not finish the house in time, he cannot expect to be paid in full, even if he had a legitimate reason for not finishing the job. He did not fulfill the terms of the contract to produce a functioning building by a fixed date, [so he has to suffer a loss].

However, an employer who wishes to test a prospective employee's dependability, and therefore sends him on an assignment for that reason only, must pay him for his effort, even if the prospective employee is unable to reach the des-

---

14 *Avos* 2:15.
15 ibid. 2:16.

tination. Because the employer accomplished his objective of testing the fellow's character, he must pay him in full. The same is true with mitzvos. Hashem has no intrinsic need for us to fulfill the mitzvos; He only wishes to test our eagerness to observe His will. This is the premise of the saying, *You are not required to complete the task.*

CHILD OR SERVANT

The Mishnah continues: *Yet you are not free men if you withdraw from it.* The Sage's implication is that by keeping Hashem's mitzvos we become children of Hashem and thus free men, rather than servants.

These two levels of relationship—*children* and *servants*—are mentioned in the *selichos* prayer *Maran d'vishmaya* where we say, *We are Your first-born child*, and, *We are Your servant.* These levels are also symbolized in the sounds of the shofar: The staccato *teruah* sound, symbolic of adversity borne with love, is the cry of the *child*, as opposed to the broken cry of the *shevarim*, indicative of one's entire body being shattered, representing the *servant.*

Because we are unsure of our status, we blow both the sobbing sound of *teruah* and the moaning sound of *shevarim.* Since the concept of *children* or *servants* is the basis of the sounds of the shofar, we also voice this doubt in the prayer following the blowing of the *shofar*, "*Today is the birthday of the world . . . Today we stand in judgment; whether as children [of G-d] or as [His] servants,*"

HOW TO OVERCOME THE YETZER HARA

We have yet to answer the question posed above: Since women are obligated in many mitzvos, why did the

Gemara ask, "In what merit do they earn a share in the World to Come?"

The Medrash[16] says that both the *Behemos* and the *Livyasan* mentioned in *Iyov*[17] symbolize the *yetzer hara*. The *Behemos* that devour vegetation represents the *yetzer hara* of overindulging in food and delicacies. *Livyasan* personifies the *yetzer hara* of lewdness and incest. In time to come, these *yetzer haros* will cease to exist, because the spirit of impurity will be eliminated from the earth.

Referring to the *yetzer hara*, Iyov said, *Nothing on earth can compare to him*,[18] because he is impossible to resist. The verse continues, *He is the king over all the haughty*, referring to those who defy G-d. Only with G-d's help can one overcome [the *yetzer hara*], and G-d's help comes through Torah study. This thought is expressed in *Koheles*, which compares the *yetzer hara* to a mighty king who laid siege to a city, threatening to invade it. The verse says, *A poor wise man saved the city by his wisdom*. Our sages explain that *his wisdom* refers to the wisdom of the Torah.[19] But a person who lacks Torah study will find it almost impossible to resist and subdue the mighty king, the *yetzer hara*. Without the proper ammunition, how can he fight this mighty warrior?

THE EXPLANATION OF THE GEMARA'S QUESTION

The Gemara asked, "*Nashim bameh zachyan?*" This is simply translated as: "With what merit can women earn a share in the World to Come?" However, in Talmudic

---

[16] *Vayikra Rabbah* 22:7.

[17] *Iyov* 10:15; 40:25.

[18] *Iyov* 41:25

[19] *Koheles* allegorically compares the *yetzer hara* in the human body to a small town conquered by a mighty king. The poor wise man who saves the town refers to the usually disparaged *yetzer tov*.

Hebrew the word *zachyan*—from the root *zocheh*—also means "to defeat." Thus the Gemara's question should be interpreted as follows: "How can women defeat the *yetzer hara* [in order to merit the World to Come]?" Since the *yetzer hara* can only be subdued through Torah study, and women are not required to learn Torah, how can they defeat the *yetzer hara*? To this the Gemara answers: Women are essential to Torah study. They enable their husbands to learn, accepting with equanimity their long hours of solitude while their husbands are learning, and they introduce their children to the teachings of the Torah. Thus, it is as if they themselves were learning Torah, and this indirect form of Torah learning gives them the strength to resist the *yetzer hara*.

The same applies to a person who is not proficient in Torah studies. Without Torah knowledge he is at the mercy of the *yetzer hara*. He can only defend himself by applying the tried and proven method of supporting Torah scholars who learn Torah for Torah's sake. Thereby, he will gain the strength to withstand the wiles of the enemy. But he must do so with joy, not considering it a burden.

MAN'S ACTIONS AFFECT THE HIGHER WORLDS

There are three categories of transgressions. Most transgressions result from ignorance or error—a person transgresses because he doesn't know that his action is sinful. And even if he knows that the action is sinful, he does not realize how his sin affects the spiritual world of divine angels, and that all the heavenly beings are damaged by his transgression. If he knew this, he would not stop weeping, shedding copious tears over his many sins which marred the holy assembly of angels.

The angels, foreseeing man's sinful inclination protested against his creation, saying, *What is frail man that You should remember him?*[20] Knowing that man's failings would damage them, they wanted to prevent his creation. Torah learning saves man from error because he learns what to do and what not to do. He recognizes the superiority of a true servant of G-d and the mediocrity of a non-observant Jew. He values the qualities of one who fulfills G-d's will, understanding how his actions make him a partner in the work of Creation. He realizes that man's good deeds build spiritual worlds, and his wickedness destroys spiritual worlds.

The destiny of every being in the higher world is determined by the actions of man. As the psalmist puts it, *You placed everything under his feet.*[21] This thought should cause you to tremble, making you serve G-d out of love and fear. How can you not be grateful to Hashem, Who has chosen you and elevated you above all creations?

THE BANE OF CONCEIT

Although knowledge of the Torah leads a person toward perfection, his impulse toward sensuality and pride is not diminished [by his knowledge of Torah]. On the contrary, the more Torah a person has learned, the more his desire for sensuality and pride intensifies. His evil impulse makes him prideful about his wisdom and the respect he is accorded. Many Torah scholars are oblivious of this tendency. Sadly, the trend toward pride and arrogance is rampant among Torah scholars, especially the urge to outshine and criticize others, a trait rooted in jealousy and rivalry. Regrettably, pride is the root of all these evils. A person with Torah knowledge, who has delved into the profundities of Torah wisdom should be humble, recognizing the kindness

---

[20] *Tehillim* 8:5
[21] *Tehillim* 8:7

G-d has bestowed on him. But lamentably, the *yetzer hara* prevails, and the greater one's Torah scholarship is, the more conceited he may be, thinking there are only few who can match his erudition. And a really outstanding scholar might display boundless haughtiness, thinking no one is equal to him.[22] This being so, a celebrated Torah scholar who is humble should be praised more than anyone else. Since he is more vulnerable to the blandishments of the *yetzer hara,* we would expect him to be utterly conceited, [yet he defeated the evil impulse]. Moshe Rabbeinu, the greatest man who ever lived, had the strongest *yetzer hara* for arrogance, yet he was more humble than any man on the face of the earth.

SHEMA THE REMEDY FOR PRIDE

The remedy [for pride] is to focus one's thoughts on the spiritual world. Cling to G-d, having Him in mind and loving Him all the time, while ignoring everything else. How can you be prideful if you realize you are a transitory, perishable creature, whose body was created from a putrid drop and is composed of detestable matter? The thought of the Creator and the angels in their radiant glory and absolute perfection should make you feel ashamed of harboring any notion of haughtiness.

One attaches oneself to G-d by reciting the *Shema*. In the first verse of *Shema,* when you acknowledge the absolute Oneness of Hashem, visualize His Presence filling the entire existence. Realizing that you, the only creature in existence capable of mentioning G-d's Name, are standing before the A-lmighty King, how can you feel haughty?

---

[22] Rabbi Yonasan Eibeshutz suffered bitterly from unfounded criticism and scathing personal attacks from contemporary Torah scholars.

The succeeding paragraphs of the *Shema,* in which we recite the mitzvah of loving Hashem and observing His mitzvos day and night, help us feel close to Hashem. By binding the *tefillin* on our arm and head and affixing a *mezuzah* to the doors of our homes, we confirm that we attach ourselves inseparably to Hashem with all our actions and thoughts. Additionally, the *tzitzis* fastened to our garments serve as a constant reminder of the mitzvos. In this manner any feeling of pride can be eliminated.

Subduing Lustful Feelings

But the [mitzvos] do not quell your sexual desire. In fact, [Shelomoh,] the wisest of all men, the greatest and most devout of all Torah scholars, stumbled because of his sexual desire. Feelings of lust can only be overcome when you consider that ultimately man is destined to die, and the fires of passion will be doused. It is all pointless and in vain.

But it is not only on one's deathbed that passion is futile. Man experiences a semblance of death each and every day when he sleeps and all desire is gone. If he indulged himself and then fell asleep dead drunk, he won't even remember whether he experienced enjoyment or endured boredom; when he wakes up it's all the same. So what is the use of gratifying your sexual desire if everything ends in death? Shelomoh deals with this at length in *Koheles,* describing how he stimulated his body with all kinds of physical pleasure, granting himself every desire. At the end he came to the conclusion that since man is destined to pass on to his final resting place *it is all toil and a vexation of the spirit.*[23]

---

[23] *Koheles* 1:14

THE THREE CAUSES OF TRANSGRESSION

Earlier we cited the Gemara:[24] *If this loathsome fellow (the yetzer hara) takes hold of you, drag him into the beis medrash. If he goes, fine. If not, recite the Shema. If that does not help chase him away, remind yourself of the day of death.* These three options correspond to the three reasons a person sins.

If he transgresses because he is ignorant of the *halachah*, he must drag the sinner into the *beis medrash* [where he will learn the laws.] If he transgresses because of arrogance and a desire for honor, the solution is to recite the *Shema*, for reading the *Shema* eliminates all feelings of pride as we expounded earlier. If he transgresses because he is overcome by sexual craving, the sinner must be reminded of his mortality, of the day he will face Divine judgment. With these three approaches, most transgressions can be avoided.

Especially during the Days of Awe, a time of Divine favor, it is incumbent on us to do *teshuvah*, attempting to break the stranglehold of the *yetzer hara* by all possible means, either through Torah learning, *kerias Shema*, or by recalling man's mortality. Let us not waste one minute, for the Sages say: *Better one hour of teshuvah and good deeds in this world than the entire life of the World to Come.*[25]

A TRUE FRIEND

The comparison *Better one hour of teshuvah and good deeds in this world than the entire life of the World to Come* seems inconsistent. Had it said, "Better one hour of good

---

[24] *Sukkah* 52b.
[25] *Avos* 4:17

deeds in this world than many years of good deeds in the World to Come," or, "Better the pleasure and delight of the World to Come than the pleasure and delight of this world," the comparison would be symmetrical. But how can we compare an hour of good deeds and *teshuvah,* to the pleasures and delights of the World to Come?

Bear in mind that we should love G-d completely, worshiping Him with total dedication. Someone who makes his friend happy feels ecstatic. Nothing is as satisfying to him as gladdening his comrade's heart. So too, one who wholeheartedly loves G-d has the mindset of a true friend, deriving the greatest satisfaction from doing things to please Him. He is like the king's attendant who will do anything to fulfill the king's wish, even enduring bitter cold, sweltering heat, hunger and thirst.

With this in mind we can understand the saying *Better one hour of teshuvah and good deeds in this world than the entire life of the World to Come.* Doing mitzvos, which gladdens The Holy one, blessed be He, is something you cannot do in the World to Come, where mitzvos do not exist. Doing *teshuvah* and good deeds in this world brings contentment to G-d, which should gratify a person more than all the delights of the World to Come, since a true friend rates his comrade's happiness above his own joy. Thus, a true friend of G-d values mitzvos which gladden G-d, more than all the delights of the World to Come.

III: THE POWER OF TESHUVAH

The most important thing to remember during the Ten Days of *Teshuvah* is to examine one's behavior, stopping the transgressions which one has become accustomed to doing. In this connection the Gemara, expounding the verse, *Love Hashem your G-d with all your heart*,[26] says: Love Him with both your impulses, with the *yetzer tov* and the *yetzer hara*.[27]

The heart is the seat of the animal soul, the evil impulse that entices man to pursue futility. It is also the seat of man's rational soul, which stems from G-d, as it says, *He blew into his nostrils the soul of life*.[28] This is the *yetzer tov*, the impulse that urges man to do good.

THE TZADDIK

A perfect *tzaddik* subdues his *yetzer hara*, transforming it into the *yetzer tov*, turning the animal soul into the rational soul. For example, the *tzaddik* eats only for the sake of the mitzvah of maintaining his health, without savoring his food. Knowing the mystical significance of eating, the *tzaddik* understands that the food he consumes can be likened to an offering on the altar as it says, *This is the Table that is before Hashem*.[29] Accordingly, at the *tzaddik's* table the animal soul is changed into the rational soul.

The same holds true for all the tzaddik's actions. He has marital relations only for the sake of the mitzvah [of procreation]. Thus it says about Yitzchak, *Yitzchak pleaded with*

---

[26] *Devarim* 5:5
[27] *levavecha*, "with all your heart" is written with a double letter *beis*, alluding to the two opposing impulses in your heart.
[28] *Bereishis* 2:7
[29] *Yechezkel* 41:22

Hashem facing his wife.[30] During marital relations, Yitzchak's mind was focused exclusively on prayer and the fulfillment of the mitzvah.

That the *tzaddik* changes the profane into the holy, the unclean into the clean, is reflected in the composition of the incense that was offered daily in the Beis Hamikdash. When the foul-smelling *chelbenah* spice was blended into the incense it became as fragrant as the aromatic *levonah.* In a spiritual sense, the *levonah* represents the "the side of holiness," while the *chelbenah* symbolizes the "the side of evil."[31] [Thus through the incense offering the *chelbenah*—the side of evil— was elevated to the level of levonah—the side of holiness.]

In the same vein, we note that the words *chametz* and *matzah* share the letters *mem* and *tzadi*, but the third letter in *chametz* is a *ches,* while the third letter in matzah is a *hei.* The minute difference between the forms of the letters *hei* and *ches* represents the difference between the side of holiness and the side of evil.

The incense [in which the *chelbenah* became as fragrant as the *levonah*] exemplifies the transformation of the *yetzer hara* into the *yetzer tov* that is brought about by the *tzaddik.* Accordingly, if the *kohen* offering the incense was not a perfect *tzaddik* he was punished. His *yetzer hara* was not transformed into the *yetzer tov,* and his offering became an *eish zarah*, an alien fire.

A person aspiring to become a *tzaddik* must stay away from luxuries; when he pampers himself he cannot be completely virtuous and pure. The Sages[32] said, *He who adds [luxuries,] makes things worse.* The Gemara[33] also says [about the showbread]: *Every kohen received a piece of the showbread as small as a bean.* Being satisfied with a small quantity is the

---

[30] *Bereishis* 25:21
[31] Also called *sitra achra*, "the other side."
[32] *Sanhedrin* 21a.
[33] *Yoma* 39a.

most effective way of changing the *yetzer hara* into the *yetzer tov*. For the same reason it says about the incense, *You may not burn anything fermented or honey as a fire offering to Hashem*,[34] since honey denotes lavishness, as it says, *Eating too much honey is not good*.[35]

THE ORDINARY PERSON

An ordinary person follows the golden mean, appeasing his *yetzer hara*—his animal soul—by eating to his heart's content, enjoying marital relations, and satisfying his physical desires. At the same time, he gratifies his *yetzer tov* by eating only permitted food in moderation on weekdays, but eating lavishly on Shabbos and Yom Tov. He avoids gazing at other women, and does everything with restraint. In short, the *tzaddik* eats from the Tree of Life while the ordinary person eats from the Tree of Knowledge of Good and Bad, seesawing from evil to good and from good to evil.

THE RASHA, THE WICKED MAN

On the opposite side of the spectrum stands the *rasha*. Driven by his *yetzer hara*, he is motivated by selfish impulses such as pride and envy, and he provokes and exploits others. All his good deeds are done only for selfish reasons, and he believes G-d is oblivious to his egotistic motives. The *rasha*, who turns the *yetzer tov* into the *yetzer hara,* is banished from Gan Eden forever. A *rasha* who wants to do *teshuvah* and enter Gan Eden is kept out by the *keruvim*, the angels that are stationed at the east of Eden.[36]

---

34 *Vayikra* 2:11
35 *Mishlei* 26:27
36 *Bereishis* 3:24.

But G-d excavates a passage at a different location where even the *keruvim* cannot stop the repentant *rasha,* as we say in the *piyut Vechol Maaminim* on Rosh Hashanah: *G-d opens a gate to those who knock in teshuvah.*

THE BAAL TESHUVAH

The *baal teshuvah* must guard himself from falling victim to the *yetzer hara*'s allure. What is he to do? Becoming a *tzaddik* and transforming the *yetzer hara* to holiness seems impossible. Even acting like an ordinary person is out of the question for the *baal teshuvah* who may easily backslide to his erstwhile failings. Rather, the *baal teshuvah* must avoid all pleasurable experiences, eating only as much as he needs to stay alive, and turning his back on any physical enjoyment, thus separating his *yetzer tov* from his *yetzer hara.*[37] His animal soul will be cast out, and he will remain only with his rational soul. At that point the Holy One, blessed be He, will embrace him with His right Hand of righteousness.

The *baal teshuvah* is brokenhearted because his *yetzer hara* is severed from his *yetzer tov.* But it says, *A heart, broken and humbled, O G-d, You will not despise.*[38]

THE SHOFAR SOUNDS

The mixture of good and evil is manifested with the blowing of the *shofar* on Rosh Hashanah. The sounds of the

---

[37] Kabbalah teaches that in the wake of Adam's sin, good and evil intermingled in a process called *iruv.* The earth too was cursed; it would bring forth thorns and thistles (*Bereishis* 3:18,19). In the *baal teshuvah,* the *iruv* is reversed; evil becomes separated from good.

[38] *Tehillim* 51:16

shofar remind us of the three categories mentioned above: the *tzaddik*, the ordinary person, and the *baal teshuvah*. The *tzaddik*, whose heart is undivided in his devotion to G-d, is represented by the straight, unbroken *tekia* sound. The ordinary people, whose mentality is a mixture of good and evil, are exemplified by the quivering *teruah* sound, and the brokenhearted *baal teshuvah* is represented by the lamenting *shevarim*.

The numeric value of the Hebrew word for heart—*lev*—is thirty two. If you divide it by two, you obtain sixteen, which is the numeric value of the word *vay*, which means "woe", reminiscent of the brokenhearted *baal teshuvah* who cries, "*vay, vay!*"—"Woe is me, for I have sinned!"

THE MARK OF A TRUE BAAL TESHUVAH

Outlining the best way to do *teshuvah*, the Gemara[39] says: Who is an example of a *baal teshuvah*? Rav Yehudah said: If one is tempted [to commit his original transgression] again, and he has the opportunity to sin with the same woman, at the same time [of his life,][40] in the same place, and he overcomes the temptation and does not sin, [then he is a true *baal teshuvah*.]

THE MALEVOLENT MASH'CHIS

Whenever a person sins, the angel *Mash'chis* (Destroyer) settles at the site of the sin, aiming his poisonous darts at people, leading them astray. When Bnei Yisrael sinned at *Pe'or*,[41] the *Mash'chis* took up residence at that location.[42]

---

[39] *Yoma* 86b.
[40] When he is still young
[41] *Bamidbar* 25:3.
[42] *Pirkei d'Rabbi Eliezer*, ch.48.

But G-d placed Moshe's tomb opposite *Pe'or*,[43] weakening the power of the *Mash'chis*. In light of this, the *Zohar*[44] cautions against moving into a house whose previous occupants were *resha'im*. For the same reason the Gemara says a person is called a *baal teshuvah* when he resists the temptation to sin, particularly in the place where he sinned before. His sin created a destructive *Mash'chis* which resides there, and the fact that he was now saved from sinning there, proves that he is a genuine *baal teshuvah*, and The Holy One, Blessed is He, helped him avoid stumbling into sin.

G-D PROTECTS THE BAAL TESHUVAH

This is implied by the saying:[45] *In the place where baalei teshuvah stand even the perfect tzaddikim cannot stand.* A *tzaddik* does not receive as much miraculous help from G-d as a *baal teshuvah* does. This being so, a *tzaddik* who finds himself in the place [where a sin was committed] might succumb to the temptation of the local *Mash'chis*, whereas a *baal teshuvah*, sheltered under G-d's miraculous protection, escapes the *Mash'chis'* trap.

WORDS OF ADMONISHMENT

Dear brothers! Look inside your home making sure no sinful blight has sneaked in, giving the *Mash'chis* the opportunity to intrude. Speaking about sinful behavior, the prophet[46] cries out, *For a stone will cry out from the wall, and*

---

43 *Devarim* 34:6
44 Vol.2, page 3.
45 *Berachos* 34b.
46 *Chavakuk* 2:11

a sliver will answer it from the beams.[47] Wickedness opens the door to impurity. During these Ten Days let us cleanse our homes through *teshuvah*. After that, we leave our homes to enter the *sukkah* where we will dwell in the shelter of the protective shadow of faith. We must be careful not to turn the pure and holy *sukkah* into a den of sin and iniquity, G-d forbid. Men socializing with women, boys mingling with girls amid raucous laughter and silly banter, card playing, and indecent conversation surely have no place in the *sukkah*. It is very important to dwell in the *sukkah* during the day and at night. In fact, the Sages stress that one should not even take a nap outside the *sukkah*.[48] In time to come, the nations of the world who are steeped in crime and violence, will ask to be given mitzvos. In response, G-d will offer them the mitzvah of *sukkah*, [by which we demonstrate our faith in G-d,] in the hope that this will induce them to repent.[49]

EATING A LAVISH MEAL ON EREV YOM KIPPUR

Following the precept that one should do *teshuvah* in the same situation that he sinned, we can explain the Gemara[50] that says, *It is a mitzvah to eat a lavish meal on erev Yom Kippur.* This Gemara gives rise to a question: How can we eat a sumptuous meal when tomorrow we will ask forgiveness for our sins, praying to be sealed in the Book of Life? Shouldn't we rather spend the day immersed in prayer, reflecting on *teshuvah?*

---

[47] The very stones of your house testify that you built your house through iniquity.
[48] *Sukkah* 26a.
[49] *Avodah Zarah* 3a.
[50] *Berachos* 8b.

TISHRI OR NISAN

Why are Rosh Hashanah and Yom Kippur ten days apart, rather than adjacent to each other?

Tosafos[51] contrasts Rabbi Eliezer Hakalir's *piyut* for Rosh Hashanah, which implies that the world was created on Rosh Hashanah in Tishri, with his *piyut* for Pesach indicating that the world was created in Nisan. The Gemara[52] also says that we calculate the years and Adam's lifetime from Tishri, but we count the seasons from Nisan.

If we count some things from Tishri, shouldn't we count everything from Tishri? Or vice versa, if we begin from Nisan, shouldn't we count everything from Nisan?

RACING THROUGH THE ZODIAC

The Rabbis debate whether the luminaries were created in Nisan under the sign of Aries (the Ram) or Tishri under the sign of Libra (the Scales). The Medrash[53] explains that before Adam's sin, the luminaries rotated at great velocity; after the sin they slowed down markedly. The luminaries were in the sign of Aries, the first sign of the zodiac, when they were created on the eve of Wednesday. Consequently, the luminaries began their course in the zodiacal month of Nisan. [Since it was before Adam's sin] they raced through the zodiac from west to east. By Friday afternoon they arrived at the sign of Scales which is Tishri.

---

[51] *Rosh Hashanah* 27a
[52] *Rosh Hashanah* 12a.
[53] Medrash Rabbah, Bereishis 10:4.

The Solution

Therefore, we count from Nisan to determine the seasons
which are dependent on the installation of the luminaries. However, the speeding sun and moon reached the sign
of Scales which was Tishri by the ninth hour of the Friday of
creation. Therefore we count Adam's age from Tishri, for the
Friday of his creation fell in Tishri. Now everything is crystal
clear. How profound are the thoughts of our Sages!

Astronomical Calculations

The new moon became visible at the start of the sign of
Scales, in the ninth hour of Friday. Therefore the
Gemara[54] says: [Adam, and Chavah] were commanded to
sanctify the moon in the ninth hour. Since the new moon became visible on that day, it was Rosh Hashanah. This being
the case, if we calculate from the beginning of Wednesday
night when the luminaries were installed, until the ninth
hour on Friday, the luminaries traversed six signs of the zodiac in sixty-nine hours. Thus, every eleven and a half hours
they traversed one sign of the zodiac. The [speed of the luminaries did not slow down immediately after the sin be-
cause] the Medrash[55] says that Adam and Chavah were not
cursed and their sin was not counted until *motza'ei Shabbos*.
Since each sign of the zodiac passed in eleven and a half
hours, one third of the sign of Scales passed during the four
hours from when Adam was commanded about the tree until
Friday night; thus when Shabbos began, the luminaries arrived at one third of the sign of Scales, which is one third of
the month of Tishri.

---

[54] *Sanhedrin* 35b.
[55] *Yalkut Bereishis* 16.

YOM KIPPUR

Adam did *teshuvah,* which was accepted, at the onset of
Shabbos, and accordingly that Shabbos was called
Shabbos teshuvah for Shabbos defended him. Therefore, Adam
sang *A psalm, as song for the Shabbos day.*[56] The Holy One,
blessed be He, granted his plea, stretching out His right hand
to him, bestowing kindness on him. According to our calcu-
lation, this happened after one third of the sign of Scales, cor-
responding to the tenth of the month, the day we celebrate
Yom Kippur. Nowadays, the luminaries progress at a slower
pace, not arriving at one third of the zodiacal sign of Scales
until the tenth of the month. Since, what took three or four
hours at Creation now takes ten days, we observe the tenth of
the month as Yom Kippur, because G-d accepted Adam's
teshuvah when the luminaries arrived at one third of the sign
of Scales. Therefore Yom Kippur is reserved for forgiveness.

The same thing happened by the sin of the golden calf
which is a semblance of Adam's sin. Yisrael received the message of forgiveness on Yom Kippur. Yom Kippur is also called
"Shabbos of Shabbosos," for it was the Shabbos of *teshuvah.*

RECTIFYING ADAM'S SIN

Let us understand that all sinful and rebellious behavior is
rooted in Adam's original sin. He ate from the Tree of
Knowledge of Good and Bad, heeding the Serpent's enticement. This is the primary sin which we must rectify shortly
before Yom Kippur, since that was the time when Adam's
teshuvah was accepted. We said previously that true *teshuvah*
becomes evident only when the sinner had the opportunity
to sin again with the same woman at the same place, but re-

---

[56] *Tehillim* 92

sists the temptation. Were the *baal teshuvah* to avoid women altogether, we could not prove that he would not sin again if he met the woman to whom he had been attracted. The same applies to all other sins. If someone sinned by eating forbidden food, and then abstained from eating altogether, we cannot be certain he would refuse the non-kosher dish he enjoyed eating previously. But if he eats only kosher food, despite being offered a non-kosher dish, then he has proved himself to be a genuine *baal teshuvah.* He had the opportunity to sin—analogous to sinning with the same woman—but overcame the temptation.

Continuing this line of thought, the Medrash[57] says: People who refrain from eating non-kosher food put Adam to shame, because he did not abstain from eating the forbidden fruit. And so, on *erev Yom Kippur*, the day Adam sinned, we want to correct his failing. To rectify his failing of eating the fruit that Chavah handed him, we eat an abundant meal.

In general, Jews take a dim view of excessive eating and drinking, eating only in moderation. Certainly on a day as holy as *erev Yom Kippur*, we must be very careful not to overeat or become intoxicated. By refraining from overeating and from eating forbidden food, we rectify Adam's sin. This is called *teshuvas hamishkal*, "*teshuvah* by counterforce," since we are doing the exact opposite of the sin. By eating only things that are kosher beyond a shadow of a doubt and observing all possible stringencies we correct Adam Harishon's sin of taking from the forbidden fruit of the Tree of Knowledge.

THE POWER OF PRAYER

The Ten Days of *Teshuvah* should be devoted to learning Torah, the "elixir of life." But truth be told, a *baal teshuvah*—and aren't we all repentant sinners—needs prayer more

---

[57] *Bereishis Rabbah* 21:9.

than anything else. Without prayer, Torah study is not effective. We know that learning Torah in a filthy place is a disgraceful thing, and regrettably, we all are filled with the filth of sin. But through prayer, *G-d washes the filth of the daughters of Tzion.*[58]

THE SINNER'S LAMENT

The essence of prayer is submissiveness and remorse, saying, "O my soul! O my soul! How badly have I soiled you and soiled myself! You were a princess, dwelling in the lofty heights of Gan Eden, lodging in the residence of G-d. G-d sent you down to earth to preserve a multitude of people who gather sparks of holiness, releasing captives from prison,[59] purifying coarse matter, turning it into sparkling sapphires gleaming like the azure blue of heaven, so that the maiden[60] will find favor before the King of kings, the Holy One, blessed be He. But I have soiled myself and soiled you, causing you to plummet from your lofty stature to become shackled in fetters, a rose amid thorns, bereaved of splendor and glory. Your fragrance has turned to a sickening stench. Your entourage of saints has fled from you, seeing you as a leprous woman, resembling a harlot. Shame on me! What will you say when Hashem takes you to task? How will you

---

58 *Yeshayah* 4:4

59 The *Zohar* (*Bereishis* 4a), teaches that at Creation, as a result of Adam's sin, a cosmic cataclysm occurred. The vessels conveying the Divine Light to the physical world shattered, spilling sparks of holiness (*nitzotzos hakedushah*) all over the world. These holy sparks became trapped in shells (*klippos*) of impurity. It is the mission of the Jewish people to redeem these trapped sparks by performing mitzvos. For example: When a Jew makes a *berachah* before a meal the sparks trapped in the food are released through his *berachah*. When he eats meat, the sparks in the meat and those in the grass the cow ate and the soil in which the grass grew are set free and return to their status of holiness.

60 The soul

defend yourself when you are summoned to the Heavenly
Court? The announcement will ring out: 'Away, unclean
one! Away, away, don't touch her! She rejected the Master's
service! Better she should not have been created!' A stillborn
baby who never saw light is better off than you. I meant to
call you 'my sister' and benefit from your grace. Instead, my
coarse body is cursed, the image of G-d has left me. How will
I ever recover from my ruin? May Hashem have pity on me;
His mercy is great."

When a man regrets his sins, is remorseful, brokenhearted,
and contrite, G-d surely will have pity on him, and then his
Torah learning will be accepted.

THE BAAL TESHUVAH'S PRAYERS

The *Zohar*[61] raises the following intriguing question: We
know the *Shechinah* does not abide in surroundings of
hopelessness, nor does it rest in an atmosphere dominated by
the "side of evil." Therefore our prayers should be uttered in
a joyous frame of mind in order to be accepted. Yet, how is
it possible for a *baal teshuvah* to be happy? Pondering his
shortcomings, he is bound to be in a gloomy mood, brokenhearted and inconsolable. How can he pray, and how will
Hashem hear his heartrending cry?

A HEAVENLY BY-PASS

For an answer, let us turn to the Gemara[62] which explores
the passage, *My soul will cry in its hidden chambers.*[63] The
Gemara distinguishes between G-d's inner chambers and His

---

[61] *vol. 2. p. 165.*
[62] *Chagigah* 5b.
[63] *Yirmeyah* 13:17

outer chambers. In G-d's outer chambers there is no sadness, only gladness rules there; but in His inner chambers, *G-d's soul will cry*, for He shares in all of Yisrael's troubles. Clearly, prayer rising on high has to pass through the outer chambers and inner chambers on its way to G-d, Who hears prayers. The outer chambers are filled with joy; in an attempt to keep the side of evil at bay, not a trace of sadness is to be found there, since sadness, which stems from despair and darkness, emanates from Lillis, [the queen of demons]. Thus the prayer of a sorrowful person is not accepted; seemingly, the *baal teshuvah's* pleas cannot reach the inner chambers since they cannot pass through the outer chambers where gladness reigns. But when the *baal teshuvah* prays, the Holy One, blessed be He, out of His great mercy, excavates a hidden passage to the inner chambers, which bypasses the outer chambers. In the inner chambers G-d shares in his grief and sympathizes with him, accepting his prayer, since his pleas are rising from a distraught and broken heart.

THOUGHTFUL PRAYER

In light of the above, it is important for us to know what to do when we pray, so our prayers should be acceptable to G-d. Most importantly, we should recite the *Shemoneh esrei* with the proper intention, not thoughtlessly rattling off the words as people do when saying *Tehillim*.

A person is to be commended for concentrating on the meaning of the words when he recites the *Shemoneh esrei*. G-d favors such prayer more than any altar offering. Concentration on the meaning of the words does not mean focusing on the thousands of esoteric and mystic intentions in every letter of the *berachos*, which are capable of opening the gates of Heaven. Rather, one should concentrate one's thoughts on the plain meaning of the words of each *berachah* of the *Shemoneh esrei*—something every person can do.

IV: The Introduction to the Shemoneh Esrei

W hen reciting the introductory phrase of the *Shemoneh esrei*, "*Hashem, open my lips, that my mouth may declare Your praise*," reflect that G-d gave you lips to guard your mouth and tongue from saying mindless things. Close your mouth as tightly as you would a treasure chest, for is there any treasure greater than your tongue, on which life and death depends? Close your lips firmly, for the Sages say, *Nothing is better than silence.*[64] Your lips should be sealed except when you open them to do G-d's will, such as to learn Torah, pray, and speak about performing mitzvos. This thought is expressed in the verse, *Open for me the gates of righteousness, I will enter them and thank G-d.*[65] The gates are our lips, which when used to serve G-d, are the *gates of righteousness.*

This is why we preface our prayer and thanks to G-d by saying, *Open my lips and enable me to speak.* But what defense is there for a person who asks G-d to unlock his mouth for prayer, yet his mouth is always open for trivialities, inanities, jokes, lies, maligning others, telling tales, gossip, informing the authorities on others, and jabbing others with piercing words. For shame!! What will the angels say? They laugh at him, saying, "What a fool! He prays to G-d to open his lips, yet his lips are buzzing with falsehood, and humming with nonsense and deception." Take this to heart and use your lips for nothing but worthwhile speech. Then you can rightfully say, *Hashem, open my lips.* Your lips will become gates of righteousness, enabling you to thank Hashem.

---

[64] *Avos* 1:17.
[65] *Tehillim* 118:19

BOWING DOWN

As we begin the *Shemoneh esrei* we bow down when we say, *baruch ata*—Blessed are You—demonstrating our submission to G-d, acknowledging that He humbles the haughty and lifts up the lowly. For this reason we revert to an erect position before mentioning G-d's name. Additionally, we bow down to the ground, man's final resting place, reminding ourselves of our mortality, as it says, *For you are dust, and to dust you shall return.*[66] Only after returning to dust, does man's soul ascend to G-d. Therefore, the Sages said: As long as the body has not turned to dust, the soul cannot rise to heaven to be bound in the bond of life.

So too, we bow down to the ground and then rise when pronouncing G-d's name, demonstrating that until we return to dust our souls will be unable to rise to heaven.

This is why the Sages said: *If one does not bow down in the Shemoneh esrei, his spine will turn into a snake.*[67] A snake lives on dust, and when a person does not bow down toward the dust, his spine will turn into a snake which feeds on dust.

The First Berachah
SHIELD OF AVRAHAM

We begin the first *berachah* of the *Shemoneh esrei* with the words: *Blessed are You Hashem . . . our G-d, the great, powerful, and awesome G-d, the supreme G-d*. Reflecting on the greatness and might of the Holy One, blessed be He, Who has selected us to serve and worship Him and has given us His Torah even though we are lowly and miserable creatures, we cannot help but rejoice and be happy.

---

[66] *Bereishis* 3:19
[67] *Baba Kama* 16b

We continue, *Who does good deeds of loving-kindness and creates everything, Who recalls the kindnesses of the Patriarchs* . . . These words summon us to be likewise kind and compassionate toward others, emulating the ways of G-d in our small way, remembering the good things others did for us while ignoring any abuse they inflicted on us, imitating G-d who remembers mitzvos and good deeds, but overlooks sins and iniquities.

The mention of Avraham reminds us to embrace the trait of this Patriarch who was kind to all, spreading the knowledge of G-d's benevolence in the world, proclaiming G-d's Oneness, and establishing the true belief among his fellowmen. Can anyone say the words, *Shield of Avraham*, without resolving to follow in Avraham's footsteps, pitying every stranger, removing every stumbling block, accepting even the pain and distress of exile with love, as did Avraham? In spite of all his calamities Avraham remained faithful to G-d with a true and loyal heart. Think about this when reciting the first *berachah*.

The Second Berachah
REVIVAL OF THE DEAD

The second *berachah* is called the *"Berachah of the Revival of the Dead."*

G-d's acceptance of a sinner's *teshuvah* has some semblance to the revival of the dead, for the Gemara[68] calls the wicked in their lifetime, dead. Thus by doing *teshuvah* the sinner is revived from the dead. However, he must pray that G-d accepts his *teshuvah*, revitalizing him with the "dew of revival." We mentioned earlier that G-d makes the dew descend without a stimulus from below [i.e., even if we have

---

[68] *Berachos* 18b.

not earned it]. And so, when we pray for dew in this *be-rachah*,[69] we should concentrate our thoughts on living in this world and being brought back to life in the World to Come. This implants in our hearts the belief that G-d will revive the dead like He promised; raising us from our graves when the world will reach perfection in the era we hope will arrive speedily in our days. Additionally, the dead coming to life reminds us of the concept that G-d created the world out of nothing.

Originally, G-d wanted to make Adam the primary creature in the world, living forever, but once he sinned, G-d said, *You shall surely die*.[70] However, because G-d's intentions last forever, man will regain the status he lost when the dead are revived, becoming the preeminent being in all of Creation, the crown of all angels on High, as it says, *Even now it is said to Yaakov and Yisrael: "What has G-d wrought?"*[71] Every Jew should anticipate this ultimate day of perfection with great joy and elation, refining his conduct as much as possible in order to become worthy of it.

The Third Berachah
THE HOLINESS OF G-D

Reciting the third *berachah, You are holy, and Your Name is holy*, a person should envision the tumultuous commotion amidst the fear and trepidation with which the angels chant, "Holy, Holy, Holy, the G-d of hosts, the whole world is filled with His honor." Reflecting on how the angels prepare themselves before they chant, he should think, "How dare I pronounce G-d's holiness without fear and trepida-

---

[69] *Mashiv haruach umorid hatal*, He makes the wind blow and He makes the dew descend.

[70] *Bereishis* 4:17

[71] *Bamidbar* 23: 23

tion? How can I utter the words, *You are holy,* without cleansing myself from sin?"

When you articulate the phrase, *You are holy,* resolve to sanctify G-d's great Name in the world, by being ready to sacrifice your life for the sake of G-d and His Torah rather than transgress even the minutest Rabbinic ruling. One should long for the opportunity to sanctify G-d's Name as the angels do, and to be a faithful witness, by giving one's life and blood, testifying that Hashem is the One and Only, and that His Torah is the Truth.

Abstaining from Things that Are Permitted

One should also reflect on sanctifying himself from things that are permitted, as the Medrash says: Hashem gave two sanctities to Yisrael and one remained for G-d alone. The word *kadosh,* "holy" means "separated from the rest," as in, *Sanctify to Me every firstborn,*[72] which means separating the firstborn from the other animals in the herd. In the same vein it says, *Since I am holy, you must [also] make yourselves holy and remain sanctified,*[73] which Ramban[74] interprets: A person should not indulge day and night in permissible delights such as meat, wine, fish, fat geese, and marital relations. Such a person is a "scoundrel with kashrus certification." Rather, the Torah tells him to be holy, meaning, detached from lavishness. He should eat only as much as needed to preserve his health, and engage in marital relations only to be saved from sin and fulfill the mitzvah of fathering children. An individual like that is *kadosh,* detached from overindulging and

---

[72] *Shemos* 1:13
[73] *Vayikra* 11:44
[74] In his commentary to *Vayikra* 19:2

pampering. He fulfills the mitzvah of *Make yourself holy*. A person who does not live by this rule violates a positive mitzvah of the Torah.

There are foolish people who believe that a self-disciplined person is an ascetic, and an abstemious person is doing more than the Torah demands. They are wrong. Shunning extravagance is a mitzvah, as I have stated. Thank G-d, there are *tzaddikim* among Yisrael who live by this rule. [This is the first sanctity given to Yisrael.]

[The second sanctity given to Yisrael is more spiritual.] These holy men of a higher order are so removed from nature that they acquire mystical powers, capable of performing supernatural wonders. They are miracle workers who are not bound by the laws of nature. One such person was the prophet Elisha about whom it says, *Behold, now I know that he is a holy man of G-d*,[75] because he performed miracles and wonders.

There is yet a third and even more lofty *kedushah*. This is the *kedushah* of the Holy One, blessed be He, Who is completely detached from physicality, existing beyond time, space, or substance. He is the Primary Cause, concealed from human comprehension. [The theme of *kedushah*] is summed up in the saying: Two kinds of *kedushah* can be found among Yisrael; but Hashem is a *kedushah* that is unique and unequalled.

Meditate on embracing *kedushah* when saying the blessing of, "You are *kadosh*", avoiding lavishness, abstaining from permissible enjoyment, and joining the league of *kedoshim*.

The Fourth Berachah
GRANTING KNOWLEDGE

The introductory phrase of the fourth *berachah* of the *Shemoneh esrei*, is, *You graciously give man discerning*

---

[75] 2 *Melachim* 4:9

knowledge. We must pray for knowledge before anything else. That is precisely what Shelomoh, the wisest of all men, did when he chose knowledge and understanding rather than long life or riches.[76] Indeed, knowledge and discernment were the primary reasons for the creation of man.

MAN'S SUPERIOR WISDOM

The Medrash[77] sheds light on this: When the Holy One, blessed be He, wanted to create man, the ministering angels protested, saying, *What is frail man that You should remember him?*[78]

G-d replied, "Man possesses greater wisdom than you. When man was created, I asked him, 'What is your name?'

He replied, 'Adam.'

"Therefore, see for yourselves that he possesses greater wisdom than you."

A QUESTION

Wherein lays the superior wisdom of man? As a creature of flesh and blood he is bound to make mistakes; exposed to the vicissitudes of the elements, he develops all his knowledge from the impressions he receives through his senses, which are notoriously imperfect and unreliable. Indeed it says, *Do not rely on your own understanding,*[79] for man tends to err and blunder. In contrast, spiritual beings, residing in their heavenly abode, free from corporeal contamination, are infallible. The pure angels near G-d are shel-

---

[76] 1 *Melachim* 3:11
[77] *Bereishis Rabbah* 19:3
[78] *Tehillim* 8:5
[79] *Mishlei* 3:5

tered by wings of the *Shechinah* hovering over them. So how can man have greater wisdom than the angels? Furthermore, how does man's reply, "My name is Adam" indicate wisdom? Adam was created from "Adamah," the Hebrew word for earth, and therefore he called himself Adam. How does this answer manifest his superior understanding?[80]

G-D'S WISDOM AND GREATNESS

In the *berachah* of *Asher yatzar*, we say, *[G-d,] Who fashioned man with wisdom*. The Creator's wisdom would not be as evident had He only created sublime spiritual beings. We would expect the Infinite Primary Cause [i.e., G-d] to create an imposing and awesome angel; G-d would then be the Cause and the angel the effect, or, to put it another way, G-d would be the Creator, the angel, the created object. The Creator's wisdom is most obvious with the creation of man, when the infinite and exalted Creator of the universe blew the soul of life into the nostrils of pint-sized little man. As a speck of dust compares to the entire universe, so does man compare to the angels in heaven, [and surely we cannot compare him to] G-d, Who is beyond comparison.

In His wisdom, G-d withdrew into Himself,[81] blowing His infinite breath into Adam's ever so tiny nostrils. The act of infusing His spirit into man, despite man's coarse and earthy nature, proves the greatness and wisdom of the Creator. The Sages[82] said about this: When blowing, a person exhales something of himself. [Since G-d blew the soul into man] the soul is a part of G-d on High.

---

[80] The full answer to this question is given further under the heading: "The reason for the name Adam"
[81] A concept Kabbalah calls *tzimtzum*, "contraction," whereby G-d withdrew into Himself to create the world.
[82] *Sefer Hakaneh.*

CHANGING MATTER INTO SPIRIT

The essence of wisdom is evident in G-d's wonders. Scientists agree that chemical elements[83] can never be modified. Some alchemists profess their ability to change earth into sapphire, but their claims are all lies; their feat is accomplished by sleight of hand. In fact, there was an alchemist in Prague who claimed to a prince that in his laboratory he had changed an ordinary pebble into a diamond. On close inspection the "diamond" was found to be plain earth. The laws of nature do not allow anything to be transformed into a different substance.

However, although man's body is physical matter, his soul transforms his physicality into spirituality, turning his dust into incorporeal spirit. After death, only a small portion of the body remains in the grave. The main part of the body clings to the soul, accompanying it either to the agonies of Gehinnom or to the bliss of Gan Eden. This counters the non-believers who shriek, "What good does a *tzaddik*'s Torah study and righteousness do him? After he dies, his soul goes to Gan Eden, but his body still rots in the grave!" They are wrong! The main part of the body joins the soul for better or for worse, going either toward grief or delight. The greater the *tzaddik*, the more of his body changes to spirit. The small portion of the corpse remaining in the grave disintegrates, while the greater part joins the soul on its journey to life in the World to Come.

MOSHE'S TOMB

Because of Moshe Rabbeinu's great merit, his entire body converted to spirit, with no bodily fragment remaining

---

[83] A chemical element is a pure chemical substance consisting of one atom. As of November 2011, 118 elements have been identified.

in the grave. Because the Torah decreed, *For you are dust, and to dust you shall return*,[84] as long as the body has not completely disintegrated, the soul does not reach its loftiest heavenly elevation. Moshe's death presented a problem. Allowing Moshe's body to linger down on earth was out of the question; it had literally grown into pure soul. Foreseeing the dilemma, G-d created Moshe's tomb on the Friday of Creation, shortly before Shabbos,[85] at the hour Adam was sentenced *to dust you shall return*. The dust of Moshe's tomb is of intangible celestial composition. This explains why, *no man knows where he was buried*.[86] Since the tomb is other-worldly, man cannot discern it.

THE REASON FOR THE NAME ADAM

Philosophers, pondering how to name an object, concluded that something comprised of a major and a minor substance should be named after the major substance. If so, why is man, a composite of matter and form, body and soul, named Adam for his *adamah* (earthly) component rather than for his soul which certainly is the more important of the two? [The fact that Adam is named for his earthly component rather than for his soul] has caused many philosophers, may their sin rest on their bones, to deny the principle of the eternity of the soul.

A craftsman will name an object that he creates for its main purpose. Thus, since the purpose of an oven is to provide heat, he names it *tanur* which is a contraction of *ten ur*, "giver of heat." The main purpose for the creation of man was to transform earth into a being with a soul, raising phys-

---

[84] *Bereishis* 3:19
[85] *Avos* 5:6.
[86] *Devarim* 34:6

icality to the level of spirituality, and enabling matter to aspire to the other-worldly. Thus, Adam was named for
adamah, because the purpose of his creation was to change
adamah—tangible earth, into *ruach*—intangible spirit.

FROM SOIL TO SOUL

[W]hen the angels objected to the creation of man] G-d
countered, "Man possesses greater wisdom than
you," implying that his creation manifested greater Divine
wisdom than the creation of angels. Accordingly, we say in
the *berachah* of *Asher yatzar, G-d, Who fashioned man with
wisdom* [i.e. G-d used wisdom in creating man]. To prove
His point, G-d asked man, "What's your name?" Replied
man, "My name is Adam," associating himself with the lowly
soil [*adamah*] rather than with his soul, the Divine component of his personality. He thereby alluded to G-d's intention
of transforming matter into spirit, as I wrote above.

WHY G-D GAVE WISDOM TO MAN

[M]an was created to use his wisdom and knowledge, and
so we pray in the *shemoneh esrei: You graciously endow
man with wisdom.* G-d gave wisdom as a free gift to no creature but man. For what purpose did the Creator give wisdom
to earthbound man? To enable him to probe the secrets of
Heaven above, the mysteries of the Divine Chariot, and the
Throne of Glory; even to comprehend the mystical letter-
permutations of the Divine Names by which G-d created the
world. O, there is so much to learn, so much to gratify the
thirst for knowledge of students of the Torah—an infinite
source of Divine grace!

A Plea to Yeshivah Students

We must beseech G-d, begging Him to grant us wisdom as a free gift. Yeshivah students especially should pray that G-d give them the clarity needed to grasp the true meaning of the Torah, without falling prey to selfish motives like pride or the urge to provoke others. How can you pray for something that goes against the will of G-d? Would you ask someone for an item that is harmful to your health? Would you ask your friend to lend you a hundred guilders to buy a watchdog whose barking will not let him sleep all night? By the same token, would you ask G-d to grant you wisdom to boast about your intelligence, dominate your community, gloat over your neighbors' ignorance, and elevate yourself at your neighbor's expense, knowing that G-d strongly disapproves of all these things? Ask for insight and knowledge entirely for the sake of Heaven. Do not be like Doeg[87] and Achitofel[88] whose wisdom led them to their ruination. To them applies the verse, *For with much [false] wisdom comes much grief.*[89] Rather, pray for wisdom that is true wisdom.

Praying for Knowledge of G-d

One should also have in mind that all his children and grandchildren be Torah scholars. A teacher of Torah should pray that his students reach a high level of scholarship and piety, without being motivated by pride or the desire to

---

[87] Doeg was a chief judge in the days of King Shaul. He betrayed David, causing the death of the kohanim of Nov (1 *Shemuel* 22:19).
[88] Achitofel was the disloyal royal adviser in the days of King David who sided with Avshalom in his rebellion against David, his father (2 *Shemuel* ch.16).
[89] *Koheles* 1:18

provoke others. He should pray that knowledge of G-d increase all over the world, and that Torah scholars abound in Yisrael. Both these phenomena are portents for the coming of *Mashiach,* as the *Zohar*[90] says: The "Generation of Knowledge" of Moshe's era will arise again in the time of *Mashiach*, which is described as the era when *the earth will be filled with knowledge of Hashem.*[91]

The Fifth Berachah
TESHUVAH

The fifth *berachah* begins, *Return us, our Father with complete repentance to You.* Appeal to G-d for help in your attempt to do *teshuvah,* for without the help of G-d it is impossible to overcome the *yetzer hara,* especially for a *baal teshuvah* who has been trapped by its allure. But the Holy One, blessed be He, sets captives free, and therefore we pray for ourselves and all Yisrael, pleading that G-d give us a pure heart and the proper outlook.

Because G-d opens a gate for those who knock on it to do *teshuvah,* He instills thoughts of purity in *baalei teshuvah,* strengthening their resolve to do *teshuvah,* as soon as they feel remorse. But then—to test their determination—G-d hides His Face from them, withdrawing His outstretched helping Hand, [inflicting pain and suffering on them]. As a result, many *baalei teshuvah* revert to their sinful past. But a perfect *baal teshuvah* continues seeking Hashem wholeheartedly and unswervingly, despite anguish, calamity, and distress. There are many *baalei teshuvah* who were once wealthy and then lost their fortune, yet did not waver.

---

[90] vol. 3:22b
[91] *Yeshayah* 11:9

THE UNWAVERING BAAL TESHUVAH

In reference to *baalei teshuvah,* Shelomoh said, *My Beloved [i.e. G-d], extended His Hand through the hole.*[92] G-d extends His right Hand to welcome *baalei teshuvah* through *the hole,* the channel He excavated beneath the Throne of Glory to receive the repentant evildoer. Before doing *teshuvah* this man was a captive of the *yetzer hara,* but now he is released, able to approach the Throne of Glory through the passage which G-d made for him.

Why did this come to pass? Because, *my insides churned for Him*—the *baal teshuvah*'s heart ached over being separated from G-d, longing to return to Him.

[The text continues,] *I arose to open for My Beloved, and my hands dripped myrrh*—[The *baal teshuvah* says,] "I study the Torah, do good deeds, pray, and give charity."

The text continues: *My Beloved has turned His back on my plea and was gone*—As we said, G-d tests the *baal teshuvah,* hiding His Face from him, making him suffer.

A true *baal teshuvah* lovingly accepts this affliction, justifying his judgment, as it says, *I adjure you, O nations destined to ascend to Yerushalayim; when you see my Beloved on the future Day of Judgment, please tell Him that I endured all hardship for love of Him.*[93] Therefore, we pray for ourselves and for all Yisrael, that G-d extend His right Hand to accept the *baal teshuvah,* and even if G-d retracts His Hand, we pray that the *baal teshuvah* persist in his *teshuvah.*

---

[92] *Shir Hashirim* 5:4
[93] ibid.v. 8

The Sixth Berachah
FORGIVENESS

The sixth *berachah* begins, *Forgive us our Father because we have sinned.* Feel remorse for your past wrongdoings when you say this *berachah,* justifying G-d's judgment and the pain He has inflicted on you. Everyone experiences suffering, yet, instead of recognizing that pain is a punishment for sin, people ascribe every affliction to chance. Realize that every mishap is a punishment for a failing, and justify your suffering properly, saying, "G-d, You are right in punishing me in this lowly and deceitful world rather than inflicting everlasting shame on me in the World to Come."

SONS OR SERVANTS

Rather than just mouthing, "I am sorry", one must feel truly remorseful for his transgression. A person is still considered a son of The Holy One, blessed be He, after sinning once or twice, but after sinning repeatedly, were he to still be considered a son of The Holy One, blessed be He, he would have to be judged as a rebellious son, who is stoned on orders of the Court.[94] Therefore, G-d, in his great mercy, demotes us from the status of sons to the rank of "servants of G-d" since a servant who disobeys his master is not put to death; he is only shackled in chains or faces other punishment.

It should be noted that a person who sins two or three times is labeled a *poshei'a,*—a rebellious sinner."[95] Thus we can explain the wording of the *berachah.* We begin, *Forgive us, our Father, for we have sinned,* as sons speaking to their Father. Then we say, *Pardon us, our King, for we have rebelled,* now

---

[94] *Devarim* 21:21
[95] *Beitzah* 16b.

speaking of ourselves as servants addressing their Master—calling G-d "our King" rather than "our Father." Furthermore, as sons who sinned, we ask G-d to "Forgive us", praying for total amnesty whereby the sin is completely erased. However, as servants who rebelled, we can only say "Pardon us", because rebellion requires expiation of the sin, sometimes through suffering and often through transmigration.[96]

In light of this, when reciting this *berachah*, we must implore G-d to wipe out our sins with abundant forgiveness, refraining from punishing us with afflictions that would impede our Torah study and prayers.

The Seventh Berachah
REDEEMER OF YISRAEL

The seventh *berachah* is, *See our affliction and redeem us.* Although we pray for the redemption of Yisrael, we should not aspire to political leadership and prosperity. Of course we will receive even these benefits, because every detail of G-d's promises will be fulfilled, but this should not be our primary wish. What good are these transitory benefits to mortal man who is here today and gone tomorrow? Focus instead on attaining spiritual perfection, and above all, pray that G-d's holy Name not be disdained and disgraced by the gentiles. When the gentiles realize the fallacy of their beliefs at the time of the Redemption, and admit that Hashem, the G-d of Yisrael, is the true King of the world, we will be most joyful. That is the intent of the words, *Redeem us speedily for Your Name's sake*—for we are not worthy of Your redemption.

---

[96] *Gilgul haneshamos* is the Kabbalistic concept called transmigration or reincarnation of the soul, whereby the soul of a deceased person is sent back to earth to live in an animal or plant, or in the body of a person who will suffer in order to atone for sins the deceased committed during his previous life. (*Sefer Shaar Hagilgulim* by Rabbi Yitzchak Luria, the *Ari Hakadosh*).

Overruling the Laws of Nature

There is no distinction between nature and the supernatural for G-d; everything is governed by the rule of justice. When G-d acts with strict justice He follows the laws of nature. Therefore, the numeric value of *Elokim*—the Name of G-d which expresses strict justice—and the word *hateva*—nature—both equal eighty-six.

Although the letter of the law follows the laws of nature, G-d will mercifully override the laws of nature, performing miracles that do not correspond to the strict letter of the law. At the miracle of the crossing of the Red Sea, G-d [abrogated the laws of nature] appearing as a mighty warrior. The Jews did not deserve this miracle according to the strict letter of the law, since; the Medrash says[97] they carried an idol with them. But the Holy One, blessed be He, acting like a powerful warrior, set aside the laws of nature. With this in mind, we say, "For You are a powerful Redeemer" praying that G-d, as a powerful warrior, disregard the strict letter of the law, and redeem us by overruling the laws of nature; otherwise, burdened with sin as we are, we would not be worthy of redemption.

Ongoing Redemption

We experience miraculous redemption every single day, as we say, *In every single generation they rise up against us to destroy us, and the Holy One, blessed be He, delivers us from their hand.*[98] This redemption is an ongoing process, as David says, *[My enemies say,] "G-d has forsaken him; pursue and catch him, for there is no rescuer."*[99] The nations want to annihilate Yisrael, wiping out the offspring of Yaakov every

---

[97] *Shemos Rabbah* 41:1.
[98] *Haggadah* of Pesach.
[99] *Tehillim* 71:11

day, but G-d hears our prayers, especially our communal prayers. Mercifully, He nullifies their plans, rescuing us from their hands, and leaving them powerless to exterminate Yisrael, as He promised us.

Because G-d redeems, rescues and delivers us every day, the Sages formulated this *berachah* in the present tense, and the *berachah* concludes, "Who redeems Yisrael" rather than the future tense "Who will redeem Yisrael," or the past tense "Who redeemed Yisrael."

In these times of distress, when so many nations threaten to destroy us, we must resolve to pray with all our heart. Yisrael is standing at the brink of annihilation! At a critical time like this, how can we refrain from praying with tears in our eyes for the redemption? And when the day goes by without our enemies' plans coming to fruition, we must rejoice that G-d has listened to our pleas. Let us continuously give thanks for the past and pray for the future because of the uncertainty of every day: *In the morning you will say: "Who can give back last night," and in the evening you will say: "Who can give back last morning"*.[100]

We must have all the exiled communities of Yisrael in mind during our prayers. May G-d have mercy on them, spreading His wings over them, to help them and save them from their oppressors.

The Eighth Berachah
HEALING AND RECOVERY

Concentrate on the sick people in your city along with the invalids in all of Yisrael, when reciting this *berachah*. Bnei Yisrael are one body and one soul, so if one Jew suffers, all of us should identify with his suffering, sharing his dis-

---

[100] *Devarim* 28:47

tress, and pleading fervently for him as if he were our own child or brother. We learn this from David, whose enemies attempted to expel him from the Jewish community, faulting him for being an offspring of Ruth, a Moabite woman.[101] They maligned and defamed David, the progenitor of Mashiach—an unforgivable crime! But David responded, *But as for me, when they were ill, my clothing was sackcloth, and I afflicted myself with lashes.*[102] Following David's example, we too should pray for each and every Jew, for every Jew fulfills some of the mitzvos; and even if he is an evildoer we should pray for him, hoping that he will mend his ways upon recovery, just as G-d waits for him to do *teshuvah* until the day of his death. Were he to die without having done *teshuvah*, the totality of Yisrael would be incomplete, and the *Shechinah* does not rest on something defective.

G-d's Anger

There is yet another reason to pray for the wicked. G-d, in His fury, judges the wicked with rigorous justice at their demise, causing a sense of anger to linger in Heaven. This is why Yirmeyah prayed that the evil enemies who denied his prophetic mission be punished [only at a time that G-d's anger has already been roused,] saying, *At the time of Your anger act against them!*[103] When G-d's anger is aroused, it can spread, and the righteous will also be judged with strict, uncompromising justice. Fearful of this, David cried out, *Hashem! Do not rebuke me in Your anger.*[104] Thus, we pray that G-d's anger towards the wicked subsides.

---

[101] Yevamos 76b
[102] *Tehillim* 35:13
[103] *Yirmeyah* 18:23
[104] *Tehillim* 6:3

Healing Yisrael from the Sickness of Exile

More importantly, we pray for the Jewish community languishing in exile whose heart is sick yearning for G-d's love. This is the pain Mashiach is suffering for Yisrael's sake; his heart is likewise ill, yearning for G-d's love, as it says, *It was our ills that he bore, and our pains that he carried.*[105] Recovery from this illness requires a great deal of spiritual awakening and *teshuvah,* as Yirmeyah laments, *Your ruin is as vast as the sea; who can heal you?*[106] Eliyahu Hanavi will turn the hearts of fathers and sons to G-d, healing Bnei Yisrael, and bringing peace. When Yirmeyah cried, *Is there no balm in Gilad; is there no healer there?*[107] he had Eliyahu in mind, for Eliyahu lived in Gilad.[108]

Gilad is located at the border of Eretz Yisrael, where Lavan made a treaty with Yaakov.[109] Both Lavan and Yaakov named the place "Witness Mound", but Lavan named it in Aramaic, *Yegar Sahadusa,* whereas Yaakov gave it the Hebrew name, *Galeid.* By giving the place a profane Aramaic name, Lavan wanted to draw Yaakov into the power of evil, but Yaakov restored its *kedushah* by naming the site *Galeid,* in Hebrew, the holy tongue, which is the language uniquely fit for Eretz Yisrael, the Holy Land. Eliyahu [who came from the holy city of Gilad] is the true healer, and his healing is the cure for which we pray.

Praying for Torah Scholars

When reciting this *berachah* for healing, we also have in mind the Torah sages who lose their strength because

---

[105] *Yeshayah* 53:4
[106] *Eichah* 2:13
[107] *Yirmeyah* 8:23
[108] 1 *Melachim* 17:1.
[109] *Bereishis* 31:42

of their total dedication to Torah study. Before the sin of the golden calf, students of Torah were powerful and muscular men, but after the sin their strength waned. This is why Moshe's arms were weary, unable to carry the Tablets when he came down the mountain.

Because Torah study saps the strength of those who study it, it is incumbent on us to pray for the health and well-being of its scholars. They are the champions of the true tradition as laid down in the Oral Torah and we are deeply indebted to them. Without Torah scholars we cannot exist, so it is an important mitzvah to pray that G-d grant them youthful strength. Furthermore, our prayers raise the respect of Torah scholarship. When all Yisrael prays for the health and contentment of Torah scholars, people are inspired to become Torah scholars themselves. In fact, many wealthy people pay large sums of money, hiring Torah scholars to learn and pray for them, realizing that they are our defenders and guardians.

The Ninth Berachah
BLESSING THE PRODUCE OF THE YEAR

In this *berachah* we pray for sustenance. Eating food without praying for it makes the food loathsome. The great Kabbalist, Rabbi Moshe Cordovero,[110] would not even set the table without first praying for sustenance. Thus, it is fitting to pray in the morning for G-d's help in earning an honest living, since eating food tainted with the slightest trace of wrongdoing defiles the body and deprives the soul of nourishment. An honest meal is nourishment for the soul; by eating it you release the "sparks of holiness" trapped in the

---

[110] Rabbi Moshe Cordovero, 1522-1570, known by his acronym, Remak, was a leading Kabbalist, who lived in Tzefas. He is the author of *Tomer Devorah, Pardes Rimonim, Ohr Yakar*, and other Kabbalistic works.

food,[111] as it says, *It is not by bread alone that man lives, but by all that comes out of G-d's mouth*.[112] We therefore pray for sustenance earned by pure and ethical means.

SANCTITY OF THE MEAL

There are many ways food may be forbidden. Examples include: Non-kosher food, food that is stolen, food eaten in the company of scorners, or food eaten in mixed company, which brings on lewd thoughts. In such cases, the element of holiness contained in the food disappears, and the impurity of the food clings to the soul of the person eating it, causing him to turn away from G-d. Indeed, we often see people tending toward sinful things after a meal. Since they were not careful guarding the sanctity of the meal, the impurity of the food attached itself to them.

CONTAMINATED FOOD

Although the sanctity of Eretz Yisrael does not tolerate impurity, expelling uncleanliness as soon as it occurs, in the Diaspora, many evildoers are reincarnated as cattle or plants.[113] If a person is not careful about guarding the purity and sanctity of his meal, the spirits of reincarnated evildoers cling to him, causing him to become an evildoer himself.[114] This is what happened with Yochanan, the *Kohen Gadol*, who became a *Tzeduki* (Sadducee)[115] at eighty years of age. Occasionally we see a man who led an exemplary life

---

[111] See footnote #59.

[112] *Devarim* 8:3

[113] See footnote #96.

[114] See Arizal, *Shaar Hamitzvos, Eikev* 43.

[115] A disloyal Jewish sect during the Second Beis Hamikdash, whose members denied the validity of the Oral Torah, believing only in the Written Torah.

turn his back on Torah and mitzvos in his old age, because the soul of a wicked person, reincarnated in the food this man ate, attached itself to him.

Avoiding Entanglement

Truly, any G-d-fearing person will shake and shiver when sitting down to eat, filled with the fear of forfeiting his life in this world and the next. Shelomoh said about this, *When you sit down to dine with a ruler, know well what lies before you*.[116]

How can we avoid entangling ourselves in this predicament? When saying, "Satisfy us from your bounty," pray to G-d with total concentration, that your food is earned by honest means. G-d will listen to your prayer, preventing you from wrongdoing at your meal. A Torah scholar should think Torah thoughts during the meal. If you are not learned, think of mitzvos like giving charity, feeding the hungry, and the like. Surely, the mitzvah of inviting the poor to join you at your meals protects you from evil.

Sustenance

Pray that G-d sustain the poor, satisfying everyone's needs, especially since poverty seems to be the main cause of sin. Were people able to make ends meet, they would not transgress, as the Gemara[117] says: At the break of dawn, the wise men of Yisrael came to see David, saying to him, "Yisrael, your people, need sustenance! The entire service of G-d and their performance of mitzvos depend on it. If they earned a living they would serve G-d with all their heart." The wise men wait-

---

[116] *Mishlei* 23:1
[117] *Berachos* 3b.

ed for daybreak, believing G-d would compassionately sustain Yisrael when He contrasts the sight of idolaters praying to their graven images while Yisrael prays to G-d with all their heart.

According to the strict letter of the law, only a person who is innocent of all wrongdoing deserves sustenance. So how can we, burdened with sin as we are, expect G-d to provide our daily bread?

G-d does not sustain us as a mandated duty; rather He grants it out of His great compassion. In line with this, the Gemara[118] says: *The livelihood of a person is as difficult to provide as the parting of the Red Sea.* Why? Because man's livelihood and the parting of the sea are both Divine gifts that we do not deserve.

We pray for our livelihood in the morning, when G-d is full of mercy. And so it says, *Satisfy us in the morning with your kindness.*[119] Similarly, in the wilderness, *in the morning there was a layer of dew around the camp. When the dew evaporated there were little grains [of manna] all over the desert.*[120] This is why the wise men came to David in the morning, petitioning him for Yisrael's livelihood.

The Tenth Berachah
INGATHERING OF THE EXILES

When reciting, *Sound the great shofar* think of the ingathering of the exiles and the proclamation of freedom for Eretz Yisrael [in the Jubilee[121]] which was accom-

---

[118] *Pesachim* 118a.

[119] *Tehillim* 90:14

[120] *Shemos* 16:13,14

[121] After counting seven Sabbatical cycles, i.e., seven times seven years, the fiftieth year is the *yoveil*, Jubilee. On the Yom Kippur of that year a proclamation with the *shofar* is made whereby all Jewish slaves were freed and all debts were cancelled.

panied by the sounding of the shofar. But this also refers to
another sounding of the shofar—the shofar blast of the great
Judgment Day.

Hearing the sound of the shofar when the Torah was given,
the Jews trembled, thinking it was the shofar blast of
Judgment Day, as it says, *There was a sound of a shofar, in-
creasing in volume to a great degree . . . The people in the camp
trembled*.[122] In fact, a Jew should always imagine the sound
of the shofar ringing in his ears, the earth trembling under his
feet, and be awe-struck with the sound of the Judgment Day.

REINCARNATED SOULS

Because Yisrael is considered as one body, which includes
all reincarnated souls, we should also think of the ingathering of all reincarnated souls.[123] *Mashiach* will not
come before all the souls in the *Guf*[124] have been restored to
their source in heaven.[125] How painful is the punishment of
reincarnation! Instead of dying in peace, a person who has already lived his life is forced to return to this world of gloom
and darkness as a new-born, wrapped in the filth of dirty di-
apers, to live a life filled with trouble and misfortune. Woe to
such agony and pain!

Apropos to this, the sin of seminal emission delays the redemption, since the sparks of holiness remain imprisoned in the
shells of impurity.[126] This sin causes many other evils, as well.

---

[122] *Shemos* 19:16

[123] Souls that have been revived and condemned to a life of pain and misery to atone for sins they committed in a previous life.

[124] Lit."body;" the heavenly region inhabited by the unborn souls.

[125] *Yevamos* 63b.

[126] At the sin of Adam Harishon a cataclysmic disaster occurred whereby the
heavenly channels of holiness shattered, spreading sparks of holiness
throughout the world where they are imprisoned inside shells of impurity.
By performing mitzvos we extract the sparks of holiness from captivity. The
redemption will take place when all the sparks of holiness have been set free.

HE ASKED FOR FISH

The Gemara[127] says: *Mashiach* will not come until a sick man wanting to eat fish, cannot find any. This means *Mashiach* will not come until all the reincarnated souls have been restored to their source in heaven. The process of restoration begins with reincarnation in man and beast, and as they reach perfection they are reincarnated in the fish of the sea, which complete their purification as they are gathered. Therefore, the souls of *tzaddikim* are reincarnated as fishes.

Medical science has established that eating fish can be harmful for a sick person since fishes are cold blooded, unless the person suffers from love sickness, in which case it is appropriate since eating fish dampens ardor. The sick man asking for fish is lovesick with love of G-d, and he seeks fish hoping to connect with the *tzaddikim* reincarnated in the fish. This is why we eat fish on erev Yom Kippur. The sick man demanding fish represents the Jewish people in exile seeking the closeness of *tzaddikim*. But when *Mashiach* comes, all the reincarnated souls will be restored, and the role of the *tzaddikim* in the category of fishes will be fulfilled. This explains why *Mashiach* will not come until a sick man requests fish, and it cannot be found.

Let us pray that the exiles—including the reincarnated souls, whether they exist in the form of minerals, plants, animals, or humans—will be rectified and restored to their source in heaven.

WHY MOSHE HURRIED

When he received the Second Tablets, Moshe declared, *[Hashem] does not clear [those who do not repent], but*

---

[127] *Sanhedrin* 97a.

keeps in mind the sins of the fathers to their children and grand-children to the third and fourth generation. Moshe hastened to bow his head and prostrated himself.[128] Asks the Medrash:[129] Why did Moshe hasten? Answers the Medrash: [He hurried,] to preclude G-d from mentioning the fifth generation.

The *Zohar*[130] objects: Moshe mentioned the third and fourth generation to ease the burden on each generation, for a shared burden is lighter. Logic dictates that were G-d to keep in mind the sins of the fathers for five generations, the burden would be carried by five rather than four generations, making it that much easier for each generation! [Why then did Moshe prevent the mention of the fifth generation?]

WHY EXILE LASTS SO LONG

When Moshe mentioned *the third and fourth generation* he was referring to the third and fourth reincarnation, for no soul will be reincarnated more than four times.[131] At a soul's fourth reincarnation G-d sends it help from above along with a holy soul to help it, so no further reincarnation will take place. In His kindness, *G-d keeps in mind the sins of the fathers . . . to the fourth generation*, but not beyond the fourth generation.

Our exile is so long because all the reincarnated souls have not yet been restored to their source in heaven. When they are restored, *Mashiach* will come. Consider: If our exile is this long when souls are reincarnated four times, imagine how much longer it would last, were souls to be reincarnated five times! G-d forbid, the exile would extend until the end of the fifth millennium!

128 *Shemos* 34:7,8
129 *Medrash Tannaim, Devarim* 5:9.
130 *Vol. 2:273b.*
131 *Zohar 2*, 91b.

Therefore Moshe, foreseeing the length of the exile, and sensing that *G-d keeps in mind the sins of the fathers to their children and grandchildren to the third and fourth generation*, quickly bowed down to prevent G-d from mentioning the fifth generation, which would cause the exile to last even longer. Likewise, we pray with heart and soul that Hashem should have mercy on us and speedily send *Mashiach*.

The Eleventh Berachah
RESTORATION OF JUSTICE

In the *berachah* "Restore our Judges" we pray for the return of the Sanhedrin.[132] The Sanhedrin represents the Throne of G-d; [its seventy members] are the earthly counterpart of the seventy heavenly Courts of Justice. As long as the Sanhedrin was in power, G-d's glory hovered over Yisrael, as it says, *There will be honor for His elders.*[133] In light of this, the Rambam says that *Mashiach* will come only after the Sanhedrin is reinstated, for the *Shechinah* is present only when the Sanhedrin administers the law, as it says, *For there sat the thrones of judgment, thrones for the House of David.*[134] *Judgment* means the Sanhedrin, the place where the Oral Torah was expounded and taught, and where disputes were settled. G-d bestowed goodness on Yisrael through the Sanhedrin, and when the Sanhedrin was in power, the laws of the Oral Torah were defined conclusively, for the judges were divinely inspired; there was no difference of opinion regarding any Torah decree, as the Gemara says.[135]

---

[132] The Great Sanhedrin was the Supreme Court of Yisrael, comprising of 71 members, headed by a *nasi*, and 70 general members.

[133] *Yeshayah* 24:23

[134] *Tehillim* 122:5

[135] *Chagigah* 16a, *Tosafos* s.v. *Yosi*.

VISION OF THE FUTURE

During the era of the Second Beis Hamikdash and for a short period after its destruction, all the disciples of judges were worthy of receiving divine inspiration. Sages like Rabbi Yochanan ben Zakkai and his companions attained wondrous spiritual heights.

When Eliyahu Hanavi, who was ordained by Achiah Hashiloni,[136] will come before the advent of *Mashiach*, he will restore the Sanhedrin, ordaining the elders of the generation as its rightful members. Then he will transmit to them the Oral Torah as he received it from Achiah Hashiloni, precluding any and all dispute. Thus, as the Sages said, he will establish peace in the world, the Redemption will sprout, and the Throne of David will be reestablished.

Pray fervently for the restoration of the Sanhedrin; these judges are authorized to sentence a guilty person to flogging, which can absolve the sinner from heavenly punishment, even from *kareis*.[137] The Medrash[138] comments: If one is sentenced down on earth, he is acquitted in Heaven above. This idea is confirmed by the verse, *G-d stands in the assembly dedicated to G-d*,[139] which implies that Divine justice is suspended when the assembly of judges on earth is passing judgment.

It is well-known that the rabbis of Tzfas expended great effort to reestablish the authority of the *semichah* ordination.[140] They wished to enable judges to sentence a guilty

---

[136] A prophet who lived at the end of the reign of Shelomoh, and during the reign of Yerovam, mentioned in 1 *Melachim* 15:29.
[137] Excision of the soul; premature death
[138] *Bereishis Rabbah* 26:14.
[139] *Tehillim* 82:1
[140] Moshe ordained Yehoshua through *semichah* (*Bamidbar* 27:33.23). He also ordained the 70 elders in this way. The elders ordained their successors who, in turn, ordained their successors. According to the Rambam, this chain of *semichah* continued until the time of Hillel Hazaken, when

man with lashes, thereby freeing him from heavenly penalty. This idea is expressed when we say the words, "justify us through judgment," for through the sentence of judges on earth one is acquitted in heaven.

In this *berachah* we also pray for upright judges, for if unethical, heretical, and corrupt judges are appointed, G-d will punish them and those that appointed them. The Mishnah[141] lists the calamities that will follow in the wake of perversion of justice. But when the officiating judges are honorable men, G-d sends blessing on the land. For this reason, we link the phrases, *Restore our judges . . . and remove from us sorrow and groaning,* in this *berachah.*

The Twelfth Berachah
DENOUNCING REBELLIOUS SINNERS

When reciting *Velamalshinim*, the *berachah* denouncing rebellious sinners, we pray for the elimination of false doctrines from our midst, praying also that the transgressors become ardent believers in the Written and the Oral Torah, and that the evil cabal of sinners who defy the rulings of the rabbis who teach Yisrael be eliminated.

When saying the words, *the guilty kingdom,* pray for the obliteration of Amalek, the wicked nation that maliciously attacked Yisrael, thereby fulfilling the mitzvah, *Remember what Amalek did to you.*[142] It is our obligation to harbor a

_____

original *semichah* ceased to exist. In 1538 Rabbi Yaakov Beirav of Tzefas attempted to restore the traditional form of *semichah* through the re-establishment of a new Sanhedrin. He convened 25 rabbis from Eretz Yisrael and conferred *semichah* on four rabbis, one of whom was Rabbi Yosef Caro, the author of the *Shulchan Aruch.* However, the renewed form of *semichah* gradually ground to a halt.

[141] *Avos* 5:8
[142] *Devarim* 25:17

deep hatred against Amalek; thus we hope that any misfortune destined to befall Yisrael, G-d forbid, strikes Amalek instead.

EXILE BRINGS ABOUT OUR SINS

The Medrash[143] tells us that on Yom Kippur, G-d charges the guardian angel of Eisav with the sins of Yisrael. Complains Eisav's angel, "Why are You heaping all these sins on my head?" G-d then transfers Yisrael's sins to the angel's clothing, causing them to turn red, as it says, *Who is this coming from Edom*[144] *with sullied garments?*[145]

This Medrash gives rise to several questions. Firstly, would G-d, the Judge of the whole world, punish one person for the sins of another? Surely the sinner is the one who must pay for his failing! Secondly, Eisav's angel complains, "Why are You heaping all these sins on my head?" But this question has an obvious answer: In order to wipe out the memory of Eisav. Thirdly, what is meant by G-d transferring Yisrael's sins to the clothing of Eisav's angel, and the verse, *Who is this coming from Edom with sullied garments?*

We must understand that G-d is the true defender of Yisrael. When Yisrael sins, G-d blames the exile and persecutions for their failings. In fact, this excuse is eminently justified for sins such as robbery, violence, hatred, envy, and neglect of Torah study and prayer, which can be attributed to the exile, the cause of the Jewish community's extreme poverty. Not knowing where their next meal is coming from, they toil hard to curry favor with government officials who exploit and abuse them. It is the misery and the constant ha-

---

[143] *Tanna devei Eliyahu Zutta* 19.

[144] Edom means Eisav, *adom* also means "red".

[145] *Yeshayah* 63:1

rassment by the nations that hamper the Jews in serving G-d as they would like.

A ROSTER OF FAILINGS

Although this line of defense is valid regarding the afore-mentioned sins, how can we justify sins like ridicule, mockery, immodesty, and all sorts of immorality and frivolity between men and women? And can the exile be blamed for the desecration of Shabbos, when people ask a non-Jew to light a fire or boil a pot of coffee for them, or they talk nonsense instead of going to shul and learning Torah? And how is the exile an excuse for negligence in the mitzvos of *tefillin* and *tzitzis*, and proper decorum in shul?

MORE WRONGDOING

The Gemara[146] relates that after the destruction of the *Beis Hamikdash*, the rabbis, [as a sign of mourning,] initially wanted to forbid eating meat and drinking wine, abolish marriage, and prohibit women from wearing brightly colored dresses. However, they did not enact these rulings in order to safeguard the survival of the Jewish people, [for without marriage there would be no future generations.] In light of this, how can we indulge in luxuries; how can our wives wear precious jewelry? The rabbis said: [As a sign of mourning over the destruction of the *Beis Hamikdash*] hilarious laughter is forbidden. Yet, deplorably, you cannot find a home that does not resound with the blaring of raucous music! At first glance, we cannot blame the harshness of the exile for all these things!

---

[146] *Bava Basra* 60b.

FLOW OF HEAVENLY ABUNDANCE

However, on second thought, I think these lamentable vices can indeed be blamed on the exile. *The Shechinah is with us in exile, suffering along with us.*[147] When the *Beis Hamikdash* was standing, G-d sent His flow of abundance to Yisrael, while dispensing a small portion to the nations of the world. But after the destruction of the *Beis Hamikdash*, G-d channels the flow of abundance to the guardian angel of the nation where Jews are in exile, and this angel conveys our share to us. In our present-day exile G-d placed our share of the abundance in the hands of the guardian angel of the nation of Eisav in whose land we are in exile. The angel of Eisav receives the heavenly abundance, passing some of it to us. No doubt, the angel of Eisav keeps the largest and best part of the abundance for himself, delivering only a tiny fraction of it to us.

THE REASON FOR YISRAEL'S SHORTCOMINGS

The *yetzer hara* is thriving, and without G-d's help it is almost impossible to resist its pull. When the *Beis Hamikdash* was standing and we received the flow of abundance directly from G-d, Yisrael's purity, piety, wisdom and knowledge grew by leaps and bounds. G-d helped us to subdue our inclination toward defilement, making it easy to observe the mitzvos. But now, the heavenly abundance flows to the guardian angels of the diverse nations who grab the bulk of the blessings, handing us the scraps, which does not give us enough strength to stand firm in the war against the *yetzer hara*. Weak and frail as we are, the *yetzer hara* captivates us, and as a result, we stand covered with sin from head to toe. Because the nations take the bulk of the heavenly abundance, they have great philosophers, scientists, and physicists;

---

[147]Tanna Debai Eliyahu Rabba ch,18,; Tosafos *Sukkah* 45a, s,v. *ani vaho.*

even the righteous gentiles among them stem from that source. In time to come, when G-d will cease funneling the abundance their way as He has promised, their wisdom will fade, as it says, *I will eradicate wise men from Edom and understanding from the mountain of Eisav.*[148]

In conclusion, there are two reasons for the downturn in Torah observance in the exile. Firstly, the exile itself prevents us from fulfilling many mitzvos and is the cause of many transgressions. Secondly, the pittance of blessing from G-d's abundance that the angels of the nations dole out to us, leaves us weak and infirm, unable to resist the lure of the *yetzer hara*.

ALL SINS DUE TO THE EXILE

Now we can understand the Medrash stating that G-d places the sins of Yisrael on Eisav. Because the bitter exile of Eisav causes Yisrael to sin, their sins are Eisav's fault. Eisav's angel counters, "Master of the universe! Perhaps I am the cause of some sins [such as theft, envy, and the decline in Torah learning], but You cannot blame me for other sins [like immorality and mockery, etc.]." G-d replies, "These sins are also due to the exile. You pocket most of the heavenly abundance that is sent through you, passing only a meager portion to Yisrael, so they are unable to withstand the temptations of the *yetzer hara*."

YITZCHAK STRIKES A BARGAIN

This helps us understand another Gemara[149] in which Yitzchak strikes a bargain with G-d, saying, "I'll take half the burden of Yisrael's sins and You'll take the other half."

---

[148] *Ovadiah* 1:9
[149] *Shabbos* 89a.

Part of Yisrael's sins can be attributed to the harshness of the exile; the other sins are caused by the nations who withhold Yisrael's share of Divine abundance. In Yitzchak's blessing to Eisav he said, "*When your complaints mount up, you will throw his yoke off your neck,*[150]" giving Eisav the strength [to oppress us] in this bitter exile. But it was G-d Who diverted Divine abundance to the angel of Eisav. Thus, Yitzchak said, "I'll take half of the burden of Yisrael's sins," for [by blessing Eisav] he caused the hardship of the exile. Yitzchak continued, "and You'll take the other half," because G-d redirected the flow of Divine abundance [making Yisrael vulnerable to the wiles of the *yetzer hara.*]

With that in mind we pray that G-d withdraw His abundant flow of holiness from the nations, returning it to us, as we had it in the past.

The Thirteenth Berachah
BLESSING THE RIGHTEOUS

When reciting this *berachah* we pray for the well-being of the *tzaddikim* (righteous), who are the source of our contentment. As long as there are *tzaddikim* in the world, there is blessing, goodness, and life in the world. It is especially important to pray for the well-being of righteous converts, loving them in fulfillment of the mitzvah, *Love the convert.*[151] This is especially true today when we live in a world of darkness and falsehood. The convert, despite our present despised circumstances, recognized G-d, like Avraham Avinu who illuminated mankind with the light of the truth. We must surely love him, kissing the ground on which he walks. The more one loves the convert, the more he loves G-d and His Torah, since this is why he converted.

---

[150] *Bereishis* 27:40
[151] *Devarim* 10:19

CONVERTS

It is important to pray fervently for the converts' happiness, praying also that G-d grant them a pure heart to keep them from backsliding in the face of the oppression and persecution of the exile. Avraham was told to go into exile in order to gather converts, as it says, *Avram took . . . the people that they had converted to G-d's cause.*[152] Likewise, the Gemara[153] says: *Yisrael was dispersed among the nations is order to gather converts*, since whatever happened to Avraham happens to his offspring.

With the words *We will not be ashamed, for we trust in You,* we pray not to suffer shame in the World to Come when we stand before A-lmighty G-d. Surely it does not refer to shame in this world, for how important is shame in this world, and for how long does it endure? A mortal man is here today and gone tomorrow. Shame and honor both last no longer than a fleeting shadow, a memory sunk in oblivion. Things are different in the World to Come. There, a sinner stands disgraced and embarrassed before the Creator, humiliated by all the angels. An announcement goes forth throughout the heavenly realm, "Away, away, don't touch this fellow who transgressed the Master's decrees! Better he hadn't been born. Pity him and pity his soul!" Angels of destruction grab him and the souls of his relatives cry bitterly, "Woe to you! What have you done, bringing this shame and disgrace on us! Why have you given us a bad name? Woe is us, how disgraceful to have a son like this!" This never ending scene is true shame and degradation. How true are Akavyah's words:[154] *I'd rather be called a fool all my life than be a wicked man for one hour in the eyes of G-d!*

---

[152] *Bereishis* 12:6
[153] *Berachos* 3a.
[154] *Avos* 5:6.

The Fourteenth and Fifteenth Berachos
Rebuilding Yerushalayim and
The Glory of Salvation

There is no need for lengthy commentaries on these *bera-chos.* Suffice it to say that we must pray passionately to G-d for the rebuilding of Yerushalayim and the return of the Davidic dynasty, which represent the ideal of human perfection. Without Yerushalayim under Davidic rule, life is not worth living. Yerushalayim is called "G-d's throne," and David's throne was a semblance of the Divine Chariot, as it says, *Shelomoh sat on the throne of Hashem as king in the place of his father David.*[155] If the angels bewail the destruction of Yerushalayim day and night, how can we remain silent? We must also cry over the desecration of G-d's name through the destruction of Yerushalayim and the loss of the Davidic dynasty. Every Jew should say in his heart, "Master of the universe! I pray that You rebuild Yerushalayim and cause the kingship of David to sprout so that Your Name is sanctified. Have mercy on your oppressed and dispersed children who suffer for sanctifying Your Name. If I am not worthy to witness the rebuilding of Tzion and the return of the House of David, I am prepared to die, ready to offer my life for the sake of Your holy Name."

The destruction of the Beis Hamikdash and the loss of the House of David have harmed us, causing us to plummet from life to death. But the opposite will happen when G-d will return the captives of Tzion; then we will rise from death to life, as it says, *When Hashem will return the captivity of Tzion we will be like dreamers.*[156] There is no need to elaborate; whoever has a Jewish soul is saddened over the destruction of Yerushalayim and the loss of the reign of the House of David.

[155] 1 *Divrei Hayamim* 29:23
[156] *Tehillim* 128:1

The Sixteenth Berachah
LISTENING TO OUR PRAYERS

The fifteenth *berachah* is *Shema Koleinu—Listen to our voice*. We must focus on the fulfillment of all our needs, big and small, when saying this *berachah*. No request is out of bounds. If you need a suitable match for yourself, your son, or your daughter, pray to G-d; if you need success in business, pray that G-d guide you in the right direction. Needless to say, if you suffer domestic discord, you certainly should pray for relief. By the same token, if there is an up-coming joyous occasion in your family, pray that nothing go wrong. Formulate your prayer in your own words, even if you stutter or cannot speak Hebrew. G-d values such heart-felt personal prayers as if they were couched in poetic phras-es, pronounced with clear articulation.

SPONTANEOUS PRAYER

G-d answers voluntary personal prayers since they are surely said with intention, unlike prayers that are said routinely and out of habit. If a person prays for something he needs at that moment, putting his wishes into words, he will concentrate his thoughts, which is the essence of the mitzvah of prayer, namely pleading from the depth of one's heart, as it says, *From the depths I called You, Hashem*.[157] One who prays spontaneously has internalized that our destiny is not determined by chance, luck, or coincidence which make prayer irrelevant. He realizes that G-d evaluates every man's deeds, and success is not the result of diligence and hard work; no man bruises his finger here on earth unless it was so decreed in heaven.[158] Any harm that strikes him is

---

[157] *Tehillim* 130:1
[158] *Chullin 7b*

from G-d, and likewise any profit or delight coming his way
is from G-d. Thus he understands that he must obey G-d's
laws, for He guides everything with close supervision.
Cheating will not help him amass wealth, for if G-d doesn't
want him to have it, no amount of drudgery and toil will
help. Furthermore, one would not ask G-d to grant him
wealth and then use it to anger Him. For example, when
someone prays to G-d for a suitable match, and then his wish
is granted, and he marries, he will certainly not follow a path
of indecency. When G-d blesses him with children, he will
not raise them to become corrupt, adopting the immoral
ways of society. He will not keep his sons away from Torah
study, nor guide his daughters toward indecency. Would a
person ask his neighbor, for money with which to torment
him? Similarly, would anyone ask G-d for a gift with which to
anger Him? Thus, a person who prays to G-d for all his needs
will not easily slide into sin, as David said, *Commit your way
to Hashem, trust in Him, He will do it.*[159]

The Seventeenth Berachah
RESTORATION OF THE DIVINE PRESENCE
TO TZION

The seventeenth *berachah* asks Hashem to favorably accept our prayers and sacrifices. During this *berachah,*
imagine lying bound on the altar as a burnt offering, ready
to offer your life in the service of G-d. In order to become
an altar offering one must be flawless. Were he to sin with
any limb, it would render his sacrifice unacceptable until he
does *teshuvah.* Indeed, all the preceding *berachos* and prayers
serve as a preparation for *teshuvah,* removing any blemish
from our soul, as it says, *When you present a blind animal for
sacrifice is nothing wrong? And when you present a lame or sick*

---

[159] *Tehillim* 37:5

animal is nothing wrong? Present it, if you please, to your governor. Would he be pleased or show you favor?[160] Thus, one should desire to be killed sanctifying G-d's Name, for with this death, we become faultless, with all our sins gone.

Pray for the restoration of the Divine service to the *Beis Hamikdash*. The Creator of the universe derives pleasure from the offerings, which brings *a satisfying aroma to Hashem*, yet they are missing! How can we rest and relax when our precious treasure has been captured? *For this our heart is ill, for these our eyes are dimmed; for Mount Tzion which lies desolate, foxes prowl over it.*[161] With broken hearts let us pray for the restoration of the Divine service to Yerushalayim; it is the fulfillment of all ideals.

When reciting the phrase, *May our eyes behold when You return joyously to Tzion*, bear in mind that one will not see the splendor of this miracle unless he is personally worthy; one cannot rely on the merit of his ancestors for this. That is why Lot's wife, who escaped Sedom only in the merit of Avraham, was not allowed to see its downfall.[162] But G-d pledges that in time to come Yisrael will be redeemed in their own merit, as it says, *For You are our Father; though Avraham may not know us, and Yisrael may not recognize us, You Hashem are out Father, "our Eternal Redeemer" is Your Name.*[163] Yisrael will merit redemption because we endured a bitter exile, lovingly accepting its affliction, believing in G-d's Oneness, and anticipating the ultimate salvation, as was the case in Egypt, when Yisrael was redeemed in the merit of their faith and trust. And so it says, *With their own eyes they will see that Hashem returns to Tzion.*[164] Accordingly we pray, *May our eyes behold Your return to Tzion in compassion.*

---

[160] *Malachi* 1:8
[161] *Eichah* 5:18
[162] *Bereishis* 19:26
[163] *Yeshayah* 63:16
[164] *Yeshayah* 52:8

The Eighteenth Berachah
THANKSGIVING

With the *berachah* of thanksgiving we offer praise to G-d for His constant miracles, even though we are usually unaware of them.[165] Many miracles are performed daily for every Jew without him knowing it, as it says, *[Give thanks] to Him who alone performs great wonders*,[166] implying that only G-d knows of the miracles and wonders; no one else is aware of them. If not for G-d's miracles we would have perished long ago, G-d forbid. All the constellations and guardian angels of the nations fight against us, as it says, *Many battle me on high*.[167] Additionally, we are obligated to offer our thanks and praises to G-d for the return of our soul each day. The *Zohar*[168] explains: Just as a person gives security to his neighbor for a debt he owes him, so too, we entrust our souls to G-d every night. And just as He returns our souls to us every morning, without keeping them for the debt we owe Him through our multiple sins, we learn not to hold on to our neighbor's security even if his debt is unpaid. Indeed, keeping your neighbor's security shows a lack of faith in G-d.

The Nineteenth Berachah
PEACE

Pray for peace, the vessel that holds blessing, the wonderful bond that unites Yisrael. Pray that discord, jealousy, and rivalry among Jews depart, and that all Jews love one another in perfect unity, harmony, brotherhood, and compan-

---

[165] *Niddah* 31a.
[166] *Tehillim* 136:4
[167] *Tehillim* 56:3
[168] *Zohar*, vol.3:119.

ionship, embracing each other as one all-encompassing soul. Have in mind that you wish to fulfill the mitzvah of *Love your neighbor as you love yourself*,[169] which encompasses the entire Torah. Pray for humility and forbearance, for if anger reigns there cannot be peace.

A PUZZLING GEMARA

The Gemara[170] relates: [At first the kohanim raced up the ramp of the altar, and the first one to reach the top four cubits won the right to do the service.] Once, two kohanim were tied running up the ramp. As they came within four cubits of the top, one thrust a knife into the other's heart, killing him. Hearing this, Rabbi Tzadok declared, "It says, *When a corpse is found fallen in the field . . . the elders of the city closest to the corpse must bring a female calf . . . and break the neck of the calf*.[171] On whose behalf shall we offer the *eglah arufah*,[172] on behalf of the city of Yerushalayim, or on behalf of the Courtyard of the *Beis Hamikdash*?"

Asks the Gemara: "Can the community of Yerushalayim bring an *eglah arufah*? Surely it has been taught that Yerushalayim never brings an *eglah arufah*!"

Answers the Gemara, "He only said this to increase weeping."

How did Rabbi Tzadok expect to increase weeping with these words?

To answer we must explain why no *eglah arufah* was brought in Yerushalayim. We must also understand why the

---

[169] *Vayikra* 19:18

[170] *Yoma* 23a.

[171] *Devarim* 21:1-9

[172] If a corpse is found on the road, we assume the murderer came from the closest city. That city must go through the process of *eglah arufah*, where a calf is brought and its neck broken as atonement.

Gemara[173] says: If the corpse was found outside *Eretz Yisrael*, near the border, they didn't bring an *eglah arufah* from *Eretz Yisrael*.

NO ANGER IN ERETZ YISRAEL

The Gemara[174] relates that when Ulla went [from Babylonia] to Eretz Yisrael, he was joined by two men, one of whom killed the other.

Rabbi Yochanan asked, "The verse *There Hashem will give you an infuriated heart*[175] refers to Babylonia. [Thus, how can a Jew in Eretz Yisrael become so angry that he slew someone?]"

Ulla replied: "This incident happened before we crossed the Yardein into Eretz Yisrael."

Anger and fury are typical for the lands outside Eretz Yisrael, but it cannot flare up in a holy place, since it only thrives in a defiled environment. Thus it says about the angels: *They are all beloved, they are all flawless; there is no envy or rivalry among them*. Correspondingly, in a holy place down on earth there is no anger. When the Torah speaks of a place where Jews will have an *infuriated heart*, it must refer to Babylonia. That is why Ulla explained, "When this happened we had not yet crossed the Yardein into Eretz Yisrael."

Now we can understand why they did not bring an *eglah arufah* in Eretz Yisrael, even if a corpse was found close to the border outside Eretz Yisrael. It is assumed that the murderer must be from outside Eretz Yisrael for someone from Eretz Yisrael would not have become so angry as to slay him and we therefore do not bring an *eglah arufah* from Eretz Yisrael.

---

[173] *Sotah* 44b. *Nedarim* 22a.
[174] *Nedarim* 22a.
[175] *Devarim* 28:65

The More Holiness the Less Anger

The more saintly a person, the more loving and complete-ly devoid of anger he is. Since Yerushalayim is the holiest city in Eretz Yisrael, the people of Yerushalayim are the most gentle of all people. The spirit of brotherly love prevailing in Yerushalayim is expressed in the saying:[176] In Yerushalayim no one ever said to his fellow, "There is not enough room for me to stay overnight in Yerushalayim," for their love of one another was so great. Since anger was uncommon in Yerushalayim, if a slain man was found near Yerushalayim, it was taken for granted that he was killed by someone not from Yerushalayim. The spirit of holiness, love, and affection that prevailed insured that the perpetrator was not a resident of Yerushalayim. By the same token, if a corpse was found and the murderer came either from Yerushalayim or from the Courtyard of the Beis Hamikdash, we assume he came from Yerushalayim, for the Courtyard has more holiness, and we know that the more holiness there is, the less anger there is.

Tragic Reversal

All this was true when holiness prevailed in the Beis Hamikdash, and sin had not taken hold there. But once sinfulness gained the upper-hand, the *Shechinah* departed, and the side of pollution took over. As a result, holiness and love were replaced by anger, as the Gemara[177] says: *Kohanim are angry men.* By nature kohanim are gentle and compas-sionate, completely free of anger; like Aharon, they pursue peace and harmony. But due to our sins everything is re-versed, and the Courtyard of the Beis Hamikdash became a site of frequent killings, as Yosef ben Gurion relates in his

---

[176] *Avos* 5:8.
[177] *Bava Basra* 109b.

book.[178] Yeshayah bemoans this, describing Yerushalayim as, *Righteousness lodged in it, but now murderers!*[179]

As a result, the question "Should an *eglah arufah* be brought if a corpse is found in the Courtyard of the Beis Hamikdash?" remains unanswered.

RABBI TZADOK'S IMPASSIONED SPEECH

The impending catastrophe of the destruction of the *Beis Hamikdash* prompted Rabbi Tzadok to fast for forty years.[180] Seeing anger provoking a kohen to murder in the Courtyard, he sensed the departure of the *Shechinah,* perceiving that the Beis Hamikdash had been defiled and the place of righteousness had turned into a den of murderers. Trying to inspire the people, Rabbi Tzadok cried out: "In case of doubt, we took it for granted that the murderer was from Yerushalayim, for the Courtyard's great holiness eliminated anger there. But now that the *Shechinah* has departed and holiness is gone, angry men and murderers abound there. Thus, the question about bringing an *eglah arufah* is still open. Let all Yisrael cry for this!"

The saintly Rabbi Tzadok's rousing speech made a deep impression. He declared that G-d left Tzion, and He is no longer its King, therefore anger and murder are spiraling. His words brought the people to tears as they conjured up a vision of havoc and destruction, which, sad to say, did indeed come true.

---

[178] Flavius Josephus, also called Yosef ben Mattisyahu (37-c.100 c.e.) was a historian who recorded Jewish history with special emphasis on the first Jewish-Roman war which led to the Destruction of the Beis Hamikdash. His most important work was *The Jewish War.*
[179] *Yeshayah* 1:21
[180] *Gittin* 56a.

A Plea for Love, Peace, and Teshuvah

Therefore let us pray that anger be replaced by love, brotherhood, and peace, which signals an increase in devotion among us, for the greater the devotion among us, the more peace and love, and less anger and divisiveness we will have. This is echoed in the saying,[181] "*The scholars of Eretz Yisrael treat each other generously when engaged in halachic debates, whereas the scholars of Babylon hurt each other's feelings when discussing halachah.*"[182] Thus let us pray that G-d establish His residence among us, blessing us with peace. That is why we conclude the *shemoneh esrei* with these words, "For those who curse me, let my soul be silent," hoping to diminish anger and hostility and increase the feeling of holiness. In that spirit we ask forgiveness from one another on *erev Yom Kippur*, pledging to strive for love and avoid anger, for this is a sign of holiness.

This is the primary intention of the *Shemoneh esrei* which every Jew is required to recite. This is especially important during these ten days when everyone must examine his behavior, remembering to do *teshuvah*. Everyone can do *teshuvah*, attaining the loftiest level of perfection. Don't despair, saying, "I have too many sins. How can I do *teshuvah*?" That is the *yetzer hara*, who, seeing someone attempting to do *teshuvah* discourages him by saying, "How can you possibly do *teshuvah*! Better enjoy life in this world; your share in the World to Come is lost anyway." That is the *yetzer hara*'s mission, but an intelligent person pays no attention to his claim. Your destiny is in your own hands. Nothing can deter you from doing *teshuvah*.

---

[181] *Sanhedrin* 24a.
[182] There is considerably more controversy in the Babylonian Talmud than in the Yerushalmi Talmud.

V. Rabbi Elazar ben Dordaya's Teshuvah

The Gemara[183] relates that Elazar ben Dordaya admitted that there was not a prostitute in the world he had not visited. One day, a certain prostitute told him that even if he repented, his *teshuvah* would never be accepted. Hearing this, he sat between two mountains, crying out, "O, you hills and mountains, please pray for me!"

They replied, "How can we pray for you when we ourselves are in need of prayer, for it says, *For the mountains will move and the hills will shake.*[184]

He then exclaimed, "O, sun and moon, please pray for me!"

They answered, "How can we pray for you when we ourselves are in need of prayer, for it says, *Then the sun will be ashamed, and the moon will be abashed.*[185]

He then cried out, "O heaven and earth. Please pray for me!"

They answered, "How can we pray for you when we ourselves are in need of prayer, for it says, *The heavens will dissipate like smoke, and the earth will wear out like a garment.*[186]

He then cried out, "O stars and constellations, please pray for me!"

They replied, "How can we pray for you when we ourselves are in need of prayer, for it says, *All the hosts of heaven will dissolve.*[187]

Finally he said, "I see that it is up to me alone." He then placed his head between his knees and wailed bitterly until

---

[183] *Avodah Zarah* 17a.
[184] *Yeshayah* 51:6
[185] ibid. 24:23
[186] ibid. 51:6
[187] ibid. 34:4

his soul departed. A heavenly Voice was heard proclaiming, "*Rabbi* Elazar ben Dordaya is destined for life in the World to Come!"

When Rebbi[188] heard this story, he cried, saying, "There are some who earn eternal life only after many years, yet here is a person who earned it in an instant!"

This gives rise to a question: Why did Rebbi cry? On the contrary, he should have been happy to see G-d's kindness in instantly granting Rabbi Believer ben Dordaya eternal life, after having lived a life immersed in immorality.

The prostitute wished to arouse Elazar ben Dordaya's lust, telling him, "Once you have sinned you can't undo your transgression. What's done is done. You can forget about a share in the World to Come, so you might as well enjoy life and have a good time in this world!" But instead of listening to her, he began analyzing the nature of sin, wondering what causes a person to sin. At first he thought that evil spirits are the root of sin, as it says, *Let a thousand [demons] encamp at your side and a myriad at your right hand.*[189]

The Gemara[190] says that demons surround a person like a ridge around a field. These diabolic spirits influence people to transgress G-d's laws. Who can resist them? It is known that they live in inaccessible mountains and hills, which is why the idolaters worship their deities on mountaintops. In fact, you can hardly find a mountain that has not been a site of idol worship,[191] since the spirits of defilement hide there. That prompted Rabbi Elazar ben Dordaya to appeal to the mountains and hills, saying, "Please pray for me, for you are the ones that made me sin." They told him he was mistaken; they had no power to cause man to sin against his creator, for

---

[188] Rabbi Yehudah HaNasi.

[189] *Tehillim* 91:6

[190] *Berachos* 6a.

[191] *Avodah Zarah* 48b.

what are they to go against the word of G-d. On the contrary, G-d's word endures forever, whereas they will perish, as it says, *For the mountains may be moved, and the hills may falter.*[192] This is confirmed by the Medrash,[193] stating, *In time to come, the Holy One, blessed be He, will overturn every place where Yisrael sinned, so there will be no reminder of Yisrael's shame.* This proves that the hills and mountains have no power to make a person transgress against his will. After all, what are they compared to G-d?

HEAVEN AND EARTH

Next Rabbi Elazar ben Dordaya thought his sin was due to the conflicting influences of heaven and earth. Science has established that opposite forces, acting on the same body, produce negative results. Since heaven and earth affect man with opposite forces, one spiritual, the other physical, the result is disruption in nature. Thus he attributed his rebelliousness to heaven and earth, thinking that due to their conflicting influence, he was born stained and corrupt. Heaven and earth replied, "We cannot nullify G-d's decree; we ourselves are destined to expire, as it says, *The heavens will dissipate like smoke, and the earth will wear out like a garment, but My salvation will be forever.* So you see it is not in our power to cause man to rebel against G-d whose rulings are irrevocable."

STARS AND CONSTELLATIONS

Next he thought his fate was determined by the stars and constellations, thinking that the stars [under whose sign

---

[192] *Yeshayah* 54:10
[193] *Sifrei Haazinu* 306.

one was born] determine whether a person will be righteous or wicked. He assumed that one's destiny was written by the stars and was unalterable. At first, he associated birth and conception with the sun and the moon, as the philosophers have it. Iyov says the same thing, *Lost be the day that I was born, and the night that it was announced, "a man was conceived,"*[194] associating birth with day and the sun, and conception with night and the moon. Accordingly, he attributed his sin to the sun and the moon. They gave him the same answer, "We cannot nullify G-d's decree; we ourselves are doomed to perdition, as it says, *The moon will be humiliated, and the sun will be shamed.*" The reason [for the ruin of sun and moon] is, as I stated above, so that Yisrael will not be embarrassed for having worshipped them. From this it is obvious that it is not in their power to negate G-d's commands.

THE CONSTELLATIONS

Having been turned down by the sun and the moon, he thought to blame the twelve constellations of the zodiac for his sin, believing there is a relationship between astronomical phenomena and events in the human world. Astrologers attribute a person's character to the stars, which determine whether he will be good, pursuing wisdom and ethics, or bad, indulging in luxuries and lewdness. But the constellation gave him the same answer; they are unable to negate the commands of G-d, for they too are destined to pass from the scene.

At birth, man is given a free will by G-d; no power in the world can force him to do either good or evil. Man alone chooses the path he wants to follow doing good or bad. G-d

---

[194] *Iyov* 3:2

has placed two roads before him, and nothing impels him to choose one or the other, except his own free will. When Rabbi Elazar ben Dordaya finally recognized that he himself was responsible for his actions, and that he had rebelled against G-d's will without anyone forcing him to do so, he ruefully placed his head between his knees, crying until his soul departed. It was then that a Heavenly Voice declared that he was destined for life in the World to Come.

A BURNING QUESTION

Why did he die immediately after doing *teshuvah?* The answer is contained in the verse, *Behold, He cannot have faith even in His holy ones.*[195] With Rabbi Elazar ben Dordaya's strong *yetzer hara,* it was possible he would revert to his sinful ways were he to continue living. Since G-d wants the best for His children, he took his life immediately, while he was still doing *teshuvah.* If G-d knows that were a person to live longer he would transgress, he has him die and instantly earn a share in the World to Come. However, when G-d sees that the longer one will live the more Torah he will learn, and the more good deeds he will perform, he will earn his share in the World to Come only after a lifetime of piety and devotion. Rebbi Elazar ben Dordaya cried because he realized that he could not be sure of himself; although he did *teshuvah* today it was possible to backslide into sin and vice tomorrow. It is understandable that he wept, unsure of what the new day would bring. It dawned on him that man is vulnerable to the *yetzer hara* every minute of the day, G-d forbid. Indeed, this thought brought Shelomoh to tears, moaning, *The day of death is better than the day of birth.*[196]

---

[195] *Iyov* 15:15
[196] *Koheles* 7:1

In light of this, a person should arouse himself to do *teshuvah* when he still has the stamina to overcome his *yetzer hara*, praying to G-d for help in subduing its blandishments. G-d's Right Hand is extended to *baalei teshuvah*, giving them a pure heart and the proper outlook to resist the *yetzer hara*'s enticement. G-d will answer the prayer of the *baal teshuvah*; He will not spurn it.

So let us pray to G-d that He send us His help from His holy abode, bringing us back in perfect *teshuvah*, and we will return as of old.

YEAROS DVASH

SIXTH *DERASHA*
TEN DAYS OF REPENTANCE
5505/1744

Sixth Derasha*

I. THE TWO GOATS

The Gemara[1] explains that the two goats, placed before the Kohen Gadol during the Yom Kippur service, were identical in size and appearance. The Kohen Gadol drew lots to determine which goat would be offered as a sin-offering and which would be sent to Azazel.[2] Because this procedure seems bizarre and incomprehensible, it requires clarification.

TAMING THE YETZER HARA

For explication let us turn to the Gemara,[3] which states that the Men of the Great Assembly cried in a loud voice, "Woe, woe! The *yetzer hara*, the evil impulse of idolatry has destroyed the *Beis Hamikdash* and driven the Jewish people into exile, and he is still frolicking among us!" They fasted for three days and three nights, until a note, inscribed with the word *Emes*—Truth—fell from heaven. Rabbi Chanina said, "From here we learn that the seal of the Holy One, blessed be He, is *Emes*". At that moment, the form of a fiery lion came out of the Holy of Holies and the prophet Zechariah exclaimed to the Jewish people, "That apparition is the *yetzer hara* of Idolatry. Grab him!" As they grabbed him, they pulled out a hair from his mane, and he cried out,

---

* We have only translated the end of this *Derasha*
[1] *Yoma* 66b
[2] A desolate place in the desert where it was pushed over a precipice to its death, symbolically carrying the sins of Yisrael with it.
[3] *Yoma* 69b

causing Eretz Yisrael to shudder. The Men of the Great
Assembly worried, "What shall we do? Maybe, G-d forbid,
Heaven will have mercy on him!" They placed the *yetzer
hara* in a leaden vessel, sealing the opening with lead to muffle the sound of his voice.

The Men of the Great Assembly also prayed to be freed
from the *yetzer hara* of sexual desire, and this too was granted to them. When they realized the world would end without this impulse [because life is not propagated without sexual desire] they darkened his eyes, [i.e. they curbed the sexual *yetzer hara*'s unbridled passion] and let him go. Because
of this, the *yetzer hara* no longer entices people to commit
incest.

QUESTIONS

This Gemara is bewildering in many ways. To begin with,
most philosophers and sages believe the *yetzer hara* is an
immaterial force of evil within the body, rather than something existing outside the body. If so, how can it be grabbed?

Even if the *yetzer hara* were an independent evil angel
whose goal is to lead people astray, the question still remains,
because an intangible spiritual being cannot be seized and
grasped, and no coarse matter can hold him captive. How
can the *yetzer hara*, a resident of the heavenly realm, be re-
strained in a leaden box?

The story of the note, inscribed with the word *Emes,*
falling from heaven sounds even more bewildering. *Emes* is
the seal of G-d, but the note did not reveal if Yisrael's request
[to do away with the *yetzer hara*] was granted. Furthermore,
it is inconceivable that the form of a fiery lion [which was the
yetzer hara of idolatry] would emerge from the Holy of
Holies. Can Satan, the epitome of impurity, dwell inside the
Holy of Holies?

THE MYSTERY GROWS

That one hair of the *yetzer hara*'s mane was pulled is also puzzling. If the *yetzer hara* is a spiritual being, how can one of its hairs be pulled out? Furthermore, can pulling one hair be legitimate grounds for such an outcry that all of Eretz Yisrael should shudder? Even if such an outcry was justified, why did the Jews fear Heaven would have mercy on him? It is unthinkable that G-d will have compassion on the wicked. When Shaul had compassion on the Amalekite children and flock, a heavenly Voice declared, "Don't be overly righteous. It is forbidden to have pity on the wicked." Indeed, the prophet says, *Hashem is vengeful to His adversaries.*[4] G-d forbid that He has mercy on [the *yetzer hara,*] this evildoer who caused the *Beis Hamikdash* to be destroyed. Yet, if the Jews were afraid [G-d would pity him], why did they put him in a leaden box and seal the cover with lead? Lead cannot muffle sound, smothering the cries of the *yetzer hara*. And if lead could make the box soundproof, would that prevent G-d from hearing his cries? Doesn't Yonah say, *From the belly of the grave I cried out—You heard my voice?*[5]

WHY DARKEN HIS EYES?

Darkening the eyes of the *yetzer hara*, so he no longer entices people to commit incest, is even more mystifying. Why would his weakened eyesight cause the *yetzer hara* to tempt a person to sin with strange women, yet not with a close relative? A lovesick person is like a sightless man, blind to reality; why should he yield to the charms of a strange woman and not to the allure of a close relative?

---

[4] *Nachum* 1:2
[5] *Yonah* 2:3

Indeed, this Gemara seems so odd, non-Jewish writers wrote books ridiculing its theme. *See O Hashem, and behold what an object of scorn I have become.*[6]

ORIGINS OF IDOLATRY

The *yetzer hara* of idol worship has its origin in faulty scientific and philosophical theories. The Rambam explains[7] that the primitive people in the generation of Enosh[8] foolishly believed that G-d, in His glorious majesty, apportioned some of his dominion to the stars and heavenly constellations [allowing them to be worshipped]. They could not grasp the concept of a Creator who is the Prime Cause of all existence, nor the principle that G-d grants prophecy to a human being. The thinkers of that era declared that the world always existed and would continue along its natural course; there is no ruler of the universe; and prayer is irrelevant. People invented theologies to suit their desires.

INTELLECTUAL ARROGANCE

Conceitedly, they thought themselves capable of discerning the essence of creation, the evolvement of heaven and earth, and the laws of nature. They denied anything they could not understand, stating, "We only believe things we understand with our intellect. The human mind is man's only guide and the ruler of his conduct." Man is made of dust, created from a putrid drop, controlled by the vagaries of the times, exposed to the changing elements, and possessed of a fickle mind, says one thing today, and the opposite tomor-

---

[6] *Eichah* 1:11
[7] *Hilchos Avodah Zarah* 1:2
[8] Son of Sheis, grandson of Adam Harishon

row. It is surely the pinnacle of arrogance for man to say, "My mind can determine matters of divinity," when he does not even know if the smallest star in the firmament consists of fire or an obscure fifth element. Furthermore, researchers of academic science often tamper with test results to prove baseless assumptions, all the more reason to mistrust doctrines on lofty metaphysical matters.

TORAH THE WAY OF LIFE

The spread of spurious beliefs was due to neglect of Torah study. People studied the holy Torah that Moshe placed before the Children of Yisrael and realized how many miracles and wonders happened to Yisrael. At first the Children of Yisrael were reluctant to believe in G-d, since their minds were corrupted by idolatry and heresy. But after witnessing manifold open miracles, they realized their previous mindset was based on falsehood.

Thus, we realize not to rely on our mental faculties. [The history of mankind confirms this, for] from the time of Enosh, [Adam's grandson in whose lifetime people began to worship idols,] until the Giving of the Torah, many scholars and thinkers enjoyed tranquil, long lives, with leisure to meditate and contemplate, free from worry, anguish, or anxiety, since the world was blessed with abundance and affluence at that time. Yet despite these advantages, they did not discover the perfect way of life. For example, Bilam and the Egyptian sorcerers were eminent scholars and brilliant intellectuals, yet they were depraved in character and morally corrupt.

The Torah is G-d's gift to those who know Him. It teaches that the opinions of secular scholars on matters of religion are worthless. The Sages of the Torah, the bearers of our heritage, are our heroes and champions. The secular philosophers with their absurd outlook on life are toiling in vain.

HUMILITY

When Moshe, the greatest prophet and sage of all time, was baffled by a problem, [he did not rely on his own reasoning] but humbly asked G-d for an answer. At times he was corrected through Aharon or Elazar's advice because a wise man does not take pride in his wisdom. If you immerse yourself in the study of the Torah and the mitzvos, you will be replete with grace, honor, humility, and piety. Recognizing the profundity of the Creator's plans to benefit all his creations, you will appreciate how deep His thoughts are and how remote they are from our thoughts. Our limited minds cannot possibly conceive His knowledge and His thoughts, as the foolish idolaters of old thought they could do.

The Torah helps those who study it for its own sake, by offering them the proper outlook, saving them from being entrapped by heretical ideas, and preventing the Satan from misleading them. *For the mitzvah is a lamp, and the Torah is light.*[9]

DECLINE BECAUSE OF NEGLECT OF TORAH

In the days of the first *Beis Hamikdash,* the Sanhedrin, the Torah sages and their disciples were prodigious Torah luminaries. However, regrettably, the common people, totally absorbed in tending their farms and vineyards, were uneducated and ignorant of Torah. Indeed, during the short period of the Babylonian exile they forgot to observe Shabbos, the fourth of the Ten Commandments, to say nothing of the other laws of the Torah. Because the masses in Eretz Yisrael were totally devoid of any knowledge of Torah, they were misled by the enticing message of false prophets, following

---

[9]   *Mishlei* 6:23

the teachings of pagan preachers. They mingled with the non-Jews, learning to pursue folly and vanity, turning a deaf ear to the voice of the prophets. Even Torah scholars were caught up with the enticements of the masses—all because of a lack of Torah learning.

ARROGANCE THE CAUSE OF DOWNFALL

Yirmeyah had this in mind when he declared, *For what reason did the land perish?—Hashem said: Because of their forsaking My Torah.*[10] They knew the land was lost because they abandoned G-d and worshipped foreign gods, yet Yirmeyah asked how did they declined to such a state of senselessness as to exchange good for evil. To which Hashem answered, *Because of their forsaking My Torah.* Their failure to learn Torah brought about their error.

The basic error of idolatry stems from arrogance, from thinking: I am smart, capable of arriving at the truth about the existence of G-d on my own.

The *Kuzari,*[11] the *Moreh Nevuchim,*[12] and similar works state that man is a replica of the *Beis Hamikdash,* and his heart, the seat of the living soul, parallels the Holy of Holies, the abode of the Tablets of Testimony. The lungs correspond to the *keruvim* spreading their wings.

THE REMEDY FOR IDOL WORSHIP

We can now explain the Gemara in *Yoma: The Men of the Great Assembly cried in a loud voice: "Woe, woe! The*

---

[10] *Yirmeyah* 9:11,12
[11] A famous work on Jewish philosophy by Rabbi Yehudah Halevi.
[12] Guide for the Perplexed, foremost philosophical work by the Rambam.

*yetzer hara, the evil impulse of idolatry, has destroyed the Beis
Hamikdash and driven the Jewish people into exile, and he is
still frolicking among us.". . . At that moment, the form of a
fiery lion came out of the Holy of Holies and the prophet
Zechariah exclaimed to the Jewish people, "That apparition is
the yetzer hara of idolatry. Grab him!"*]

The Men of the Great Assembly [who prayed to destroy
the *yetzer hara* of idol worship since it caused the destruction
of the *Beis Hamikdash*,] were afraid the Jews [returning from
the Babylonian exile to rebuild the *Beis Hamikdash*] would
fall prey once more to the scourge of idolatry [and cause the
rebuilt *Beis Hamikdash* to be destroyed.] Investigating the
matter, they found that the underlying cause of heresy is arrogance, symbolized by the fire in the Holy of Holies, which
corresponds to the heart of man. Thereupon the prophet
Zechariah told them that [pride] is the reason for all agony
and misfortune.

EMES

[*They fasted for three days and three nights until a note, in-
scribed with the word Emes—Truth, fell from heaven.
Rabbi Chanina said, "From here we learn that the seal of the
Holy One, blessed be He, is Emes."*]

The remedy [for idol worship] was shown to [the Men of
the Great Assembly] in the note that fell from heaven inscribed with the word *Emes*—truth. Truth, the seal of the
Holy One, blessed be He, symbolizes the Torah which em-
bodies the Truth. Through the truth of the Torah, the errors
of the various heresies are laid bare, helping people recognize
that Hashem is the One and Only. Thus, the note from heav-
en declared that through Torah, the *yetzer hara* of idolatry
can be eradicated.

EZRA THE SCRIBE

The Men of the Great Assembly were led by Ezra the Scribe, who transcribed a carefully edited *sefer Torah*, free of typographical errors, written with the familiar Hebrew characters, [rather than the ancient archaic script,] to be learned and taught. It was so lucid and understandable that people compared it to the Torah Moshe brought down from Sinai! Ezra also instituted that a portion of the Torah be read on Shabbos at the Minchah service for the benefit of people who missed the Torah reading in the morning service, further ordaining that ten verses of the Torah be read on Mondays and Thursdays.

GROWTH OF TORAH

The Men of the Great Assembly said: Make a fence for the Torah and develop many disciples.[13] Following their own teaching, they established Torah academies in every region, and urged every town and village to hire teachers for young children. We have suffered countless calamities and have been exiled from place to place, engulfed by fire and water, yet, thank G-d, the Torah and its rabbinical interpretations have not been forgotten. Torah study and pious devotion are growing by leaps and bounds, although attempts to entice us with heresies and idolatry are an unfortunate part of every generation. It is our Torah spirit that shatters all alien ideologies; the fire of Torah consumes the chaff of their hollow doctrines, rendering their missionaries powerless. G-d's seal is Truth, and with the Torah which is true we immobilize the power of the *yetzer hara* of idolatry, preventing him from leading us astray.

---

[13] *Avos* 1:1

PREEMINENCE OF TORAH SCHOLARS

Those who are engrossed in Torah learning are the honor guard of the royal palace, the elite of the King's ministers. Therefore, they must be extremely careful not to make the slightest error, much less a serious lapse. Indeed, the Gemara[14] says, The Holy One, blessed be He, is scrupulous with those close to Him, even for matters as seemingly insignificant as a single hair. It stands to reason; G-d is closely associated with Torah scholars, for He dwells within the four ells of Halachah. Thus, a Torah Scholar defiles the heavenly abode with the slightest error, and his inadvertent sins are considered intentional transgressions. Ordinary people, by contrast, can claim ignorance as an excuse, and their intentional sins are reckoned as accidental transgressions. A Torah scholar is held accountable for the slightest error since he is engrossed in the study of Torah, and familiar with the minute details of *Halachah.*

PRIDE AND ANGER

It is not difficult for a Torah scholar to sense some feeling of pride, which can consume him like fire. In *Avos d'Rabbi Nosson*[15] Rabbi Shimon ben Gamliel said he deserved his execution by the Romans, because he felt a tinge of pride when he gave a discourse on the Temple Mount with all the sages of Yisrael sitting before him. For him, this was a grave transgression. We should shed copious tears over this, for it is impossible for a Torah scholar to avoid feelings of pride.

A tendency towards anger, generated by the heat of Talmudic debate, can be another pitfall for Torah scholars.

---

14 *Bava Kamma* 50a
15 Chapter 38

Although feelings of anger are permitted while searching for the truth, this can cause one to get angry in other situations. The *Moreh Nevuchim* explains that Moshe's sin in striking the rock was that he spoke in anger[16] rather than in gentle terms as befits a person of his stature. This proves that anger and indignation have disastrous consequences.

G-D IS PARTICULAR WITH TORAH SCHOLARS

[*When the Men of the Great Assembly grabbed the yetzer hara, they pulled out a hair from his mane.*]

This Gemara means that the Holy One, blessed be He, is particular with those devoted to Him even in matters as trivial as a single hair, as it says, *His surroundings are exceedingly turbulent.*[17] [When the hair was pulled out] all of Eretz Yisrael shuddered, because a minor transgression was judged as a serious offense. This unnerved the Men of the Great Assembly. If a Torah scholar's most insignificant error is deemed a grave sin, there is reason to fear that G-d will easily become enraged. Satan will then have opportunity to drag the sinner into committing more serious violations, for "one sin brings on another sin." A minor infraction opens the door for the *yetzer hara* to tempt the person, who is almost powerless to resist his lure.

THE POWER OF TESHUVAH

With that in mind, the prophet Hoshea exclaims, *Return, Yisrael, unto Hashem your G-d, for you have stumbled in your iniquity.*[18] Even though your sins against

---

16 *Bamidbar* 20:7-13
17 *Tehillim* 50:3
18 *Hoshea* 14:2

G-d are manifold, *teshuvah* is effective, *for you have stumbled in your iniquity* - your main blunder was in negligently committing your first misstep, which led to the other sins. *Teshuvah* is readily accepted, for once you committed your first transgression it was almost inevitable that you would commit other sins.

FOUR KINDS OF METAL

[*T he Men of the Great Assembly said: "What shall we do? Maybe, G-d forbid, heaven will have mercy on the yetzer hara!"*]

They were afraid G-d might have mercy on the *yetzer hara* because of a Torah scholar's sin, but they found a solution to that problem.

[*They placed him in a leaden vessel, sealing its opening with lead to muffle the sound of his voice.*]

Gold, silver, copper, and lead are four primary metals which are the source of all other metals. Gold alludes to the Torah which is likened to a flaming fire, existing solely for the sake of G-d. For this reason [Torah study] is completely free of any trace of the *yetzer hara*. The same applies to the mitzvah of *tefillin*.

Silver is symbolic of white *tzitzis* which have the power to whiten and purify Yisrael like snow and wool. This mitzvah is completely devoted to G-d.

Some mitzvos are also influenced by the *nachash*, the serpent, which is the symbol of the *yetzer hara*. For example, the mitzvah of procreation, which entails sexual arousal, and eating on Shabbos and Yom Tov, require the participation of the *yetzer hara*. These mitzvos fall into the category of *nechoshes*, copper, [from the same root as *nachash*], because the *nachash* plays a part in them.

Prayer, the primary "service of the heart," is called "lead," because lead is heavy and prayer should be said with "a heavy head," i.e. deep concentration. Lead [*oferes* from the root *afar*, "dust"] is a composite of dust and air [*afar* and *avir*] and therefore melts quickly when exposed to fire. Air readily separates from dust, as air rises upward while dust sinks downward. Similarly, in prayer, we direct our thoughts upward toward heaven while aiming our eyes downward toward the earth, our final resting place. This explains why prayer is compared to lead, the combination of dust and air.

Lead is used in a furnace to purify gold and silver, since it removes all dross and contaminants leaving the gold and silver unadulterated. Ultimately, everything emanates from dust and everything returns to dust.

PRAYER PURIFIES THE SOUL

Similarly, a person's sins, whether in thought or deed, cling to his soul like dross, but when he submissively prays for forgiveness, his impurities are removed and remain in the furnace while he emerges pure and spotless. Like a furnace, prayer purifies the soul, removing the dregs of haughtiness and anger, melting one's faults with the meekness of his prayer. Prayer mitigates pride and anger in a person, since one becomes cognizant of his lowly stature and his trivial destiny when praying.

The Medrash[19] teaches that the *tamid* offering of the morning negates the sins of the night, and the *tamid* offering of the afternoon cancels the sins of the day. So too, the prayers of the morning and the evening erase all sins like a foundry removing dregs, leaving the one who prays as pure as the driven snow.

---

19 *Bamidbar Rabbah* 21:21

Morning and Evening Prayer

[*T*he *Men of the Great Assembly grabbed the yetzer hara,*
confining him in a lead vessel, sealing its opening with a
lead cover.]

They were afraid a Torah scholar might commit a minor
offense which would afford Satan, [one of the cohorts of the
yetzer hara,] an opportunity to accuse Yisrael. To prevent this
they placed him in a lead vessel, sealing its opening with lead.
This allegory implies that they instituted the morning and
evening prayers. Before the time of the Men of the Great
Assembly, prayer was not biblically ordained. In fact, according to the Rambam, prayer was required only once a day,
without a prescribed text or set time. The Men of the Great
Assembly formulated the wording of the prayers and established morning and evening as its set time. This is symbolized
by the lead furnace which purifies silver and gold, removing
all impurities.

They sealed the mouth of the vessel, for the mouth en-
ables us to speak and pray. Thus, they silenced the voice of
the Accuser (Satan), implying that a G-d-fearing person's
morning and evening prayers will cleanse him, purging his
sins. The daily prayers, said with concentration, will stifle all
accusers, cancel all unpremeditated sins and inhibit lust. By
placing Torah study and prayer on a firm footing, the Men of
the Great Assembly under the leadership of Ezra the Scribe
wiped out the *yetzer hara* of idolatry. This is their most enduring achievement.

Modesty of Women

[*T*he *Men of the Great Assembly prayed to be freed of the ye-*
tzer hara of sexual desire, and this was also granted to
them. When they realized the world would end without this im-

pulse, because life is not propagated without sexual desire, they darkened his eyes, [i.e., they curbed the sexual yetzer hara's unbridled passion] and let him go.]

They also enacted decrees to curb the strong *yetzer hara* of sexual desire that is essential for the propagation of the human race—for example ordaining[20] that a woman must wear a *sinar*—a small undergarment or apron—as a token of modesty. According to the commentators, Ezra mentioned the *sinar* as one example, but he meant that any exposed limb of a woman must be covered.

The Torah decrees that in public a woman must be dressed in a chaste and modest fashion and may not uncover her hair. In fact, Yeshayah speaks scathingly about *the daughters of Tzion walking with outstretched necks and winking eyes, walking with dainty steps.*[21] Ezra further decreed that even in the privacy of her home a woman must wear a modesty apron. Women do not usually encounter strange men in their homes, and if she has male visitors she surely is fully dressed; however Ezra ordained that a woman should dress modestly at home, so even close relatives should not see any exposed limbs.

The Men of the Great Assembly "darkened the eyes of the *yetzer hara*" by decreeing that women wear a chastity apron even in the privacy of their homes to discourage close family members from gazing at the mother of the house. In so doing, they safeguarded the sanctity and virtue of the Jewish home.

SUMMARY

Our sages wisely instructed the people to engage in the study of Torah for its own sake and to pray regularly with

---

[20] *Bava Kamma* 82a.
[21] *Yeshayah* 3:16

submissiveness and humility. Daily Torah study and prayer purify a person, removing all pollutants from his soul. The modest behavior of the Jewish woman both in public and in private, where she neither uncovers her hair or any part of her body even when she is in total seclusion preserves the purity of the Jewish home. This offers protection from the *yetzer hara* who seduces a person to view sights of indecent exposure. An accomplished woman will be saved from all these harmful influences; *she will be praised in the gates by her very own deeds.*[22]

IDENTICAL IMPULSES

[We can now clarify the reason for the procedure of the two goats brought on Yom Kippur.] In Scripture the goat is a symbol for the *yetzer hara* of idolatry and the *yetzer hara* of sexual promiscuity. Both these impulses are identical; sinning with one leads to sinning with the other, because sexual immorality is rooted in disbelief. The sinner does not care about the laws of the Torah; on the contrary, he tells himself, "G-d is not concerned with the affairs of this world; the world runs by the laws of nature." Because immorality and atheism are two sides of the same coin, with one sin leading to the other, the two goats of Yom Kippur, which symbolize these two impulses, were identical in size and appearance.

THE RED RIBBON

The goat sent into the wilderness hints at idol worship. It was expelled to a remote site in the desert where Lilith and her demons cavort, to be cast over a cliff until its limbs were scattered everywhere.

---

[22] *Mishlei* 31:31

Idolatry originates in the glib and smooth talk of the missionaries. Shelomoh compares them to *a harlot who has death on her tongue and venom between her teeth*.[23] A red ribbon—indicative of a tongue—was tied between the goat's horns. When the goat plunged to its death, the ribbon miraculously turned white, conveying the message that "life and death are in the hands of the tongue."

Babylonian Jews

The Sages exerted themselves to distance us from heresy, for its harmful ideas infect a person's body and soul. Even the thought of heresy is sinful. For this reason, *the one who sends the goat to Azazel shall immerse his body and his clothing in a mikveh, only then can he enter the camp*,[24] and whoever touches him becomes defiled. Since the Babylonian exile was caused by idol worship, the Babylonian Jews [living in Yerushalayim] knew from personal experience how much misery this goat—the symbol of the *yetzer hara of* idolatry—had caused. They would prod the goat-driver, pulling his hair, shouting: "Hurry up; get going!"[25]

Ten Sukkah-Huts

Ten *sukkah*-huts were set up along the route to Azazel,[26] reminiscent of the ten stages of holiness. For the same reason, the distance from Yerushalayim to the cliff of Azazel was ten miles. The ten *sukkah* huts along the way denote

---

[23] *Mishlei* 5:3.4
[24] *Vayikra* 16:26
[25] *Mishnah Yoma* 66a
[26] They were filled with food and refreshments to reassure the goat-driver who could not eat on Yom Kippur.

Torah which shields against heresy. At each *sukkah*-stop the goat-driver was invited, "Come in! Have some water and a bite to eat," which is indicative of Torah, as it says [regarding Torah study,] *Come and partake of my food and drink, of the wine that I mixed.*[27] The ten stages of defilement, of which idol worship is the lowest, are also alluded to with the ten miles and ten stops.

The Gemara[28] says that in the days of Ezra, Yisrael sat in *Sukkos*. In a figurative sense this means they nullified the *yetzer hara* of idolatry. This metaphor is understandable because the *sukkah* stands for Torah, and the Torah puts an end to the *yetzer hara* of idol worship. Because the authority of the Torah was reestablished in the days of Ezra, Bnei Yisrael [figuratively] sat in the *sukkah*.

CURTAILING THE BENEFICIAL IMPULSE

The goat sent to Azazel represents the *yetzer hara* of idolatry which must be wiped out. In contradistinction to this, the *yetzer hara* of passion cannot be totally crushed because its energy is needed to arouse the desire for sexual intercourse and to stir the appetite for food and drink. However, its stimulus must be used for the sake of Heaven; to have children and to fortify the body which is a miniature universe. We must preserve our health so we are physically fit to worship in the Palace of the King, the eternal G-d.

This *yetzer hara*'s vigor and stamina are personified by the goat that is slaughtered, whereby we diminish its potency and lust so we can use this impulse to fulfill mitzvos. This goat is *the goat that has the lot "for Hashem"*[29] since we dedicate this impulse to G-d, when we offer it as a sacrifice.

---

[27] *Mishlei* 9:5
[28] *Arachin* 32:2
[29] *Vayikra* 16:9

In light of this, we must keep our indulgence within bounds. We must dedicate our heart and soul to serving Hashem and His Torah, making it our priority, especially during the Days of Awe.

II. THE DAY OF JUDGMENT AND THE DAY OF REPROOF

The Medrash[30] says: Woe is us on our Day of Judgment! Woe is us on our Day of Reproof! Bilam was embarrassed by his donkey's admonition; the brothers were terribly flustered by Yosef's simple declaration, "I am Yosef," as it says, *The brothers were so startled, they could not respond.*[31] When Hashem tells us [on our Day of Judgment,] "I am Hashem," our shame will be much greater.

What is the difference between "our Day of Judgment," and "our Day of Reproof"? Furthermore, what is the connection between Bilam's donkey and Yosef's disclosure to the embarrassment we will feel on our Day of Judgment?

WHY THREE JUDGMENT DAYS?

Man is judged three times: During his lifetime he is judged on Rosh Hashanah and Yom Kippur; after his demise he is judged before the heavenly Court on the Great Judgment Day; and all creation will be judged on the Great Judgment Day when the Dead are revived. Asks Ramban:[32] Why do we need three days of judgment, instead of one definitive, final Day of Judgment?

---

[30] *Bereishis Rabbah* 93:10
[31] *Bereishis* 45:3
[32] Rabbi Moshe ben Nachman, (Nachmanides) (1195-1270), one of the greatest Torah commentators, halachists, and philosophers.

A PARABLE

Let me answer with a parable. A king sent his trusted servant, dressed in royal attire, on a mission to a distant land. While there, instead of carrying out his assignment, the servant joined a band of fun-loving drunkards, staining his royal robe with the filth of taverns and dark alleys. Hearing that his servant had misbehaved, the king punished him mildly, hoping he would be ashamed of his disgraceful conduct. The servant solemnly swore to mend his ways, but soon forgot his pledge and reverted to his loose behavior.

This time, the king arrested him and locked him in a dark dungeon, shackled in chains. Despondent, the servant wailed, "Please set me free! I will turn over a new leaf. From now on I will serve you faithfully!" The king's heart melted from his pathetic moaning and he had him released. But no sooner did the servant sense liberty than he forgot his promise, sliding back to his corrupt ways. This time the king said, "He leaves me no alternative. My last resort is summoning him to the royal palace." When he arrived at the palace, the servant was ordered to launder his garments, bathe, and cleanse his body of all stains, blotches, and smudges. Next he was told to spend several days fasting and mortifying himself, only then would he be ready for an audience with the king.

Greeting the servant, the king said, "Having cleansed yourself, you are worthy of seeing me. But justice demands that you be punished for violating my decrees. The anguish you experienced in the dungeon was not meant as punishment; it was intended to guide you on the right path. The discomfort of cleansing your body and laundering your garments was not a punishment either; it enabled you to enter the palace." Without compassion, the king sentenced the servant to punishment for dereliction of duty according to the strict letter of the law.

A Wake-up Call

This scenario happens to us on the three Days of Judgment. The Holy One, blessed be He, sent us down to earth to fulfill His mitzvah assignments. But we neglected his instructions, choosing instead to live a life of transgression and looseness. G-d disciplines us with minor afflictions for our sinful behavior as a warning to abandon our improper way of life. This happens on Rosh Hashanah, the day on which the fate of every person is inscribed.

Suffering the pain of his affliction, the sinner expresses regret and does *teshuvah*. But before long he returns to his former lax way of life. This time, G-d sends him ailments and infirmity, as a wake-up call to shake him from his illusions. He may be compared to a person who has fainted. He is slapped in the face, and a stick is inserted into his mouth breaking his teeth, not as a punishment or in revenge, rather, to stir him to consciousness. Similarly, these afflictions and ailments are intended to awaken person from his stupor and stir his soul. This is what happens to a person annually on Rosh Hashanah.

Three Days of Judgment

If a person continues to transgress, shrugging off the afflictions he has suffered, the Holy One, blessed be He, will decree death for the sinner. Although he will want to return to G-d on High, he will not be allowed to do so because his soul and body are hopelessly stained. At that point the length of time he will stay in Gehinnom, enduring the inferno of fire, snow, and other forms of torment to purify him of all contamination will be decided. At the end of this cleansing period, he will be ready to enter the King's heavenly palace. Although his soul suffered a great deal in Gehinnom, his agony is not considered punishment; rather it is a purging and purification for him.

The Great Judgment Day occurs at the end of days. The Holy One, blessed be He, will say to the sinner, "True, you have cleansed and sanctified yourself, preparing to enter the King's palace, however, the rigorous ordeal you endured is not punishment for violating G-d's commandments." At that point he will be sentenced for failing to heed all the warnings and refusing to change course from evil to good. This is the significance of the three Days of Judgment.

DAY OF REPROOF

Thus, the ultimate Great Judgment Day at the end of time is the real Judgment Day, and Rosh Hashanah, the day on which we are judged every year, is the Day of Reproof. Its aim is to admonish a person, cautioning him to forsake his wicked ways. If not for the annual warning on Rosh Hashanah, a sinner could justify himself on the ultimate Judgment Day, saying, "I sinned inadvertently; I was preoccupied with the futilities of life. I didn't know what I was doing!" But the annual Day of Reproof allows for no such excuse. During his lifetime the sinner suffered multiple mishaps and accidents cautioning him to mend his ways, but he did not pay attention to the warnings. When the call goes forth, "Woe is us on our Judgment Day," We may answer, "Why? After all, we have a good excuse. We were ignorant and oblivious." Comes the retort, "Woe is us on our Day of Reproof [i.e., your defense does not hold water for you were already warned against transgressing on Rosh Hashanah]."

THE YETZER HARA'S PLOYS

The *yetzer hara* uses two approaches to deceive us. When a person suffers a series of mishaps, the *yetzer hara* tells him, "You just had bad luck." If he lost money, the *yetzer hara* explains: "It's the economy; the whole country is suffering from the earthquake, the heat wave, the flood etc. We're all in the same boat. G-d didn't single you out."

The *yetzer hara* attributes every calamity to the forces of nature or to coincidence, and the person [who listens to the *yetzer hara*,] does not realize G-d is sending him a message to change his sinful way of life, even though he is suffering misfortune. But an intelligent person will be upset [when struck with calamity], saying to himself, "This has never happened to me before. Why today of all days?" Analyzing when and how the accident happened, he will conclude that it was a punishment for his shortcomings, especially since the Holy One, blessed be He, retaliates measure for measure, according to the gravity of the sin. Praiseworthy is the person who is aware of this.

BILAM'S MISTAKE

This explains why Bilam was embarrassed by his donkey's admonition. Finding no reason for the donkey's refusal to budge, Bilam attributed it to chance. But the donkey chided him, saying, "Don't blame it on a fluke. Have I been in the habit of doing this to you? How can you think it happened by chance? You should have taken it to heart, realizing it is a miracle!" Bilam was speechless. So too, when misfortune strikes, a person should take it to heart, reflecting, "Is this a common occurrence?" He will conclude, "No, this did not happen by chance."

THE SECOND DECEPTION

The *yetzer hara* comes up with yet another scheme. If a person swindled his neighbor, the *yetzer hara* whispers, "Were your neighbor not destined to be duped and lose money, a thousand crooks could not defraud him. Heaven decreed he should suffer a loss, and you are merely acting as G-d's agent to carry out His will. Had you not cheated him, someone else would have. So don't worry, you won't be penalized."

This line of reasoning is ridiculous. Indeed it says,[33] "Deserved good fortune is brought to good people by good people, and deserved misfortune is brought on guilty people by guilty ones." And the Gemara[34] says, "G-d wants the heart," meaning, G-d judges a person by his intentions. If your intention was to commit larceny, you will be punished.

A PARABLE

Let me illustrate this with a parable: A king was gravely ill; the greatest physicians were unable to cure him. A traitorous royal aide, bent on assassinating the king, served the king a concoction of poison and snake venom, to kill him. "Here is the medicine the doctor prescribed," the aide said. But miraculously, after taking the "medication", the king's health improved and all symptoms of his disease disappeared. The venom had acted as an antidote, reversing the cause of the disease. Would anyone think the would-be assassin should not be put to death? The same applies to the person who cheated his neighbor. Even though heaven decreed the neighbor must suffer a loss, the cheater must be punished for his crooked act.

---

[33] *Shabbos* 32a
[34] *Sanhedrin* 106b

The Lesson

The same thing happened to Yosef's brothers. When Yosef revealed himself they were terribly flustered. [But just as the king was healed through the attendant's perfidious act] so did Yosef become the viceroy of Egypt because his brothers sold him into slavery. Nevertheless, the brothers were deeply ashamed. This holds a lesson for all of us. If Yosef's brothers were embarrassed by his implied reproof, how much more so will we be embarrassed [on Judgment Day?] Don't let the *yetzer hara* entice you, saying it was G-d's will that Yosef become viceroy [and the brothers are not to blame]. Whoever commits an injustice will receive the punishment he deserves [regardless of the consequences of his misdeed].

Conclusion

This teaches us to examine our behavior and do *teshuvah*, for G-d is abundantly forgiving and the Master of mercies. *He will once again show us mercy, He will suppress our iniquities, You will cast all our sins into the depths of the sea.*[35] *A redeemer shall come to Tzion.*[36] Amein.

---

[35] *Michah* 7:19
[36] *Yeshayah* 59:20

GLOSSARY

ADAM HARISHON - Adam the first man

AHARON - Aaron

AMALEK - Wicked descendants of Eisav who attacked Yisrael when they left Egypt

AVRAHAM AVINU - Abraham our forefather

AZAZEL - The goat sent to the desert on Yom Kippur for atonement

BAAL TESHUVAH pl. *BAALEI TESHUVAH* - Penitent

BAMIDBAR - The Book of Numbers

BEIS DIN - Jewish court

BEIS HAMIKDASH - Holy Temple

BERACHAH pl. *BERACHOS* - Blessing

BEREISHIS - The Book of Genesis

BNEI YISRAEL - Children of Israel

CHAMETZ - Leavened bread

CHAVAKUK - Habakuk

DERASHAH pl. *DERASHOS* - Discourse or Sermon

DEVARIM - The Book of Deuteronomy

DIVREI HAYAMIM - The Book of Chronicles

EGLAH ARUFAH - A calf whose neck is broken as atonement for an unresolved murder.

EICHA - The Book of Lamentations

EISAV - Esau

ELIYAHU - Elijah

ERETZ YISRAEL - The Land of Israel

EREV - The day preceding a holiday

GAN EDEN - The garden of Eden

GEHINNOM - Hell

GEMARA - Talmud

HALACHAH pl. *HALACHOS* - Law

HASHEM - God

HOSHEA - The Book of Hosea

IYOV - Job

KADOSH - Holy

KAREIS - Punishment of premature death

KEDOSHIM - Holy ones

KEDUSHAH - Sanctity

KERIAS SHEMA - Recitation of the portion of the Torah
         containing the declaration of Hashem's unity

KERUV pl. *KERUVIM* - Cherubs

KOHEIN GADOL - High Priest

KOHEIN pl. *KOHANIM* - Priests, descendants of Aaron

KOHELES - Ecclesiastes

LASHON HORA - Gossip

MASHIACH - The Messiah

MATZAH - Unleavened bread

MELACHIM - The Book of Kings

MEZUZAH - Parchment scrolls containing the Shema that
         is placed on the doorpost.

MIDRASH - Homiletic interpretation of the Sages

MIKVEH - Ritual immersion pool

MINCHAH - The afternoon prayer

MISHLEI - Proverbs

MISHNAH - Compilation of the oral tradition; it also
         refers to one paragraph of this compilation

MITZVAH pl. *MITZVOS* - Commandment

MOSHE RABBEINU - Moses our Teacher

MUSSAF - The additional prayer on holidays

NISSAN - The first Hebrew month which is in the spring

ONKELOS - A convert who wrote an Aramaic translation of the Torah

PESACH - Passover

RASHA pl. *RESHA'IM* - A wicked person

SANHEDRIN - Jewish High Court

SEFER - Book or scroll

SELICHOS - Penitential prayer recited during the High Holidays

SEMICHAH - Ordination

SHABBOS pl. *SHABBOSOS* - The day of rest - Saturday

SHECHINA - Divine Presence

SHELOMOH - Solomon

SHEMONEH ESREI - The eighteen beracha prayer that we say thrice each day

SHEMOS - The Book of Exodus

SHEMUEL - The Book of Samuel

SHEVARIM - The broken sound blown with the shofar

SHIR HASHIRIM - Song of Songs

SHOFAR - Ram's horn blown on Rosh Hashanna

SHUL - Synagogue

SUKKAH - Hut used on Sukkos

SUKKOS - Festival of Tabernacles

TEFILLAH - Prayer

TEFILLIN - Phylacteries

TEHILLIM - Psalms

TEKIA - The straight sound of the shofar blast

TERUAH - The staccato sound blown with the shofar

TESHUVAH - Repentance

TISHRI - The first month of the year

TOSAFOS - Supplementary commentary to the Talmud

TZADDIK pl. *TZADDIKIM* - Pious Person

TZITZIS - Fringes worn on a four cornered garment

VAYIKRA - The Book of Leviticus

YAAKOV - Jacob

YARDEIN - The Jordan River

YERUSHALAYIM - Jerusalem

YESHAYAH - Isaiah

YETZER HARA - Evil inclination

YIRMIYAH - Jeremiah

YISRAEL - Israel

YITZCHOCK - Isaac

ZOHAR - The primary book of Kabbalah